Raising Christian Children in a Secular World

Sara,

The greatest journey you will ever take will be as a parent. May God and His word always be your guide.

Cheryl Dickow

4/05

Raising Christian Children in a Secular World

Finding Your Parental Authority in God's Word

Cheryl Dickow

Pleasant Word

Packaged by Pleasant Word, PO Box 428, Enumclaw, WA 98022. The views expressed or implied in this work do not necessarily reflect those of Pleasant Word. The author(s) is ultimately responsible for the design, content and editorial accuracy of this work.

Unless otherwise noted, all Scriptures are taken from the Holy Bible, New International Version, Copyright © 1973, 1978, 1984 by the International Bible Society. Used by permission of Zondervan Publishing House. The "NIV" and "New International Version" trademarks are registered in the United States Patent and Trademark Office by International Bible Society.

Scripture references marked KJV are taken from the King James Version of the Bible.

Scripture references marked NASB are taken from the New American Standard Bible, © 1960, 1963, 1968, 1971, 1972, 1973, 1975, 1977 by The Lockman Foundation. Used by permission.

ISBN 1-4141-0291-7
Library of Congress Catalog Card Number: 2004097300

This book is lovingly dedicated to
my husband John
who gives me strength and support in all that I do,
to my sons Jared Robert, Justin Joseph, and Jordan John
who are true blessings from God,
to my dearest friend Pam
who inspires me as a mother and as a Christian,
to my wonderful friend Kathy
whose love for her nieces and nephews reminds me that aunts are
"moms" too,
to my kind friend Vivian
whose generosity towards others is boundless,
and to the Holy Spirit
who guides me in the most amazing ways.

Dearest Parent,

Raising Christian children in a secular world is a tough task. Your work is made even more difficult because of the many and contrary outside messages that your child receives. You try to teach kindness, generosity, and gratitude while the world teaches chicanery, self-gratification, and greed.

Through it all you become inundated with mixed messages as well. Popular television hosts and self-help books become your source of guidance and wisdom. You are running in a multitude of directions and wearing as many hats as there are stars in the sky. In the end no one seems to be winning, neither you nor your child.

This small book contains nothing new because, in God, there is nothing new. His Word remains the same yesterday, today, and tomorrow. Instead, this book is a gentle reminder that your children are a gift from God and what you do with them is your gift back to God.

I simply want to encourage you to turn to God as your only true source for parental guidance and answers. Now is the time to find all the answers you have been looking for in His word and in His son. With God this journey we call "parenting" will be rewarding, joyful, and insightful.

In Christ,
Cheryl Dickow

Table of Contents

The Storm

Parenting is not for the faint hearted. Of course, by the time we parents recognize this, we are already in the thick of it: enmeshed in battles, surrounded by self-help books, and fearing for our very sanity. When our children are preschoolers we try to teach them to be independent minded, free thinking individuals. Then, before our very eyes, they become exactly what we have encouraged them to be! Much to our chagrin they push against our values and challenge our very authority. The cute independence of their preschool years becomes the bane of our existence during the middle and high school years. They develop their own ideas that are in stark contrast to the rules we so naively set up while they were still quietly ensconced in the womb.

School truly becomes a time of transition and change. As the years progress we see that our family values seem to clash with societal values. Friendships often become more important than family. Scripturally speaking, these years seem to be the storm before the calm. A time when your child is testing the waters, testing your patience, and testing your stamina. In an amazing turn of events, your once close relationship with your child may become difficult and frustrating. You begin to question your confidence in his or her ability to make decisions. Your marriage and your family life may feel the effect as you grapple with tumultuous emotions (yours and your child's) while trying to maintain sanity and decorum in your household. These turbulent pre-adolescent and adolescent years often arrive with little warning. A storm in every sense of the word: unexpected and intense. The kind of storm you want to take shelter from and watch from a safe place while it passes. However, anyone who has been through this will tell you that it seldom passes without the need to set up sandbags and batten down the hatches!

Interestingly, these times seem to be universal in the journey of life. Most importantly, they can be understood in the scripture story of Jesus helping the disciples weather a violent storm. At first dismayed by the violence of the storm, the disciples are quickly put at ease by Jesus' command of the situation. And, as we may well know, once Jesus brings his disciples past this event, they are filled with harmony and well being and are ready for the next step of their journey with Him. Consider these school years as one of your life's storms, indeed one of your child's life's storms. A storm to weather. A storm in which your child will become better equipped for the next step in life. Jesus provided us with the beautiful and appropriate example of compassionate authority. Our role as parents is to model ourselves, the best we can, after His example. As parents we want to raise our children with that same compassionate authority. Com-

He got into a boat and his disciples followed him. Suddenly a violent storm came up on the sea, so that the boat was being swamped by waves; but he was asleep. They came and woke him, saying, Lord, save us! We are perishing!" He said to them, "Why are you terrified, O you of little faith?" Then he got up, rebuked the winds and the sea, and there was great calm.
Matthew 8:23–26

I urge you now to keep up your courage; not one of you will be lost, only the ship.
Acts 27:22

passion allows us to see, know, and feel the circumstances of our child's life. Authority allows us to let our head rule over our heart to make the right decisions for our child. Compassion should be balanced with authority for both to be effective and valuable.

> *In their distress they cried to the Lord, who brought them out of their peril, hushed the storm to a murmur; the waves of the sea were stilled. They rejoiced that the sea grew calm. That God brought them to the harbor they longed for. Let them thank the Lord for such kindness, such wondrous deeds for mere mortals.*
>
> *Psalm 107:28-31*

Fortunately, to take command of the situation is as simple as turning to scripture as your guide and authority on all things. God has given us all the answers we need for this and all the storms of life. God gave us His Word. We have often heard the phrase, "What Would Jesus Do?" Learning the Word of God will always give us a correct answer to that question, regardless of the situation. All we need to do is live the Word of God. A simple desire. A daunting task.

The Word

When I was in high school in the mid 1970's there was a popular saying, "God is my co-pilot." I guess it was a way to reestablish God in the lives of many people who had turned away in the untamed 60's. And although the saying was cute I never gave it much thought. Truth be told, I never gave God much thought either. I was raised in a non-practicing Christian household. Holidays were more secular than religious. Easter was simply a time for tight curls, beautiful bonnets, and shiny white shoes. I knew very little of my savior. Instead I gingerly looked forward to the Easter goodies that were to be found at my grandmother's house. The Passion, Death, and Resurrection were but a dim backdrop for coloring eggs and visiting the Easter bunny at the mall.

So it didn't really seem to matter who the co-pilot was. Now, some 30 years later, there is an amended saying to that original one. It says, "If God is your co-pilot, you are in the wrong seat!" I love this version. Of course, I'm also in a different place in my life. A place that has brought me, on my hands and knees, to God. I am a parent. And this saying shows a clear understanding of life as a parent. It lets us know that God is the only one that can be in charge. He is the pilot. He is the ultimate parent. We are the co-pilots. The foster parents, so to speak. We play a critical role. We have an important job, vital to the flight, but secondary to the pilot. We take our instructions from Him and constantly defer to His wisdom, guidance, and decisions. He's weathered many storms and doesn't lose sight of His goal regardless of the conditions. Keeping this in mind will give us a renewed understanding of our children. For me, this means that I now have a deeper sense that my children really belong to God. And, like Joseph, I truly am the foster parent. It is no small sign of confidence that God somehow looked into my heart and deemed me fit to raise three boys for Him. Now I understand that my accounting will be how I raised these boys for Him. And there couldn't be a more rewarding or more challenging role to take on.

> *Whoever clings to me I will deliver; whoever knows my name I will set on high. All who call upon me I will answer, I will be with them in distress; I will deliver them and give them honor. With length of days I will satisfy them and show them my saving power.*
>
> *Psalm 91:14–16*
>
> *How can the young walk without fault? Only by keeping your words.*
>
> *Psalm 119:9*
>
> *With a curse you rebuke the proud who stray from your commands. Your decrees are my delight, they are my counselors.*
>
> *Psalm 119:21, 24*

Let's face it, raising children isn't always an easy or turbulent-free ride. I have had to reevaluate friendships with mothers who refused to acknowledge the difficulties of raising children. Perhaps that was their coping mechanism, but I found it difficult to be with them. And for years I allowed myself to feel inferior to these mothers. I wondered what I was doing wrong and they were doing right. However, given enough observation time, I now know that all parents have a tough row to hoe. There might be different problems, but there are problems indeed. How many times have parents joked, "Kids don't come with an instruction book!"? We all chuckle and then nod our heads in solemn agreement, "Ah, yes, instructions. They sure would be great." And so it goes, that unspoken truth that we need help. Some more than others, but all of us, in some way, are trying to find our way as parents.

But if we go back to that understanding of our role as foster parents it behooves us to make the next logical assumption. That assumption would be that God did give us an "instruction book." Does it make any sense that God would give us His most precious gift, His children, and not leave us with instructions? Of course it makes no sense. God is the God of reason, order, and well-being. And so, of course He left instructions. Powerful, authoritative instructions. Unfortunately, we are looking to be empowered in all the wrong places. We are looking to "tell-it-like-it-is" radio and television personalities and "take-no-prisoners" judges and talk-show hosts for guidance and authority. But the ultimate power has already been granted to us as parents. And it has been granted by the ultimate Father, our Father, Lord and Savior of the world. So now it's time to turn to His instructions and raise His children according to His word, pleasing to Him. Then, and only then, can our children truly be all that God intended. This is when their lives will be blessed and overflowing with graces. When we raise them according to the Word of the Lord.

But how often do we tap into this boundless resource? How often do we remember that God's Word is the first place to turn to for answers and guidance? Like so many other areas of our lives, we tend to look for instructions as a last resort. Based upon our life's experiences, we only need to consider how much easier the journey would be with directions. We attempt to get the DVD player hooked up and working by trial and error. We figure we can put the bookcase together without the illustrated instruction page. Whatever it is, we tend to try to do it on our own first. Then, when we have a big mess on our hands, we open up the instructions.

Our children are too big of a "project" to leave to trial and error. In learning scripture we will find great lessons on raising children. Scripture teaches the key lessons that will help make our children successful in life: diligence, joy, perseverance, humility, prayer, character, honesty, and responsibility to name just a few. Regardless of the stage we are at in raising our children, we will find that it is never too early, or ever too late, to open up the instruction book. Turn to God's word. Learn God's word. Find all our answers in God's word. God's Word, which is **always** available to us, is just what we need. Day or night, let us tap into His endless love, blessings, and guidance for our family.

As a middle school teacher and mother of three sons I have cherished the time and energy I have put into learning the Word of God. The Word has helped me weather many storms and has provided invaluable guidance, peace of mind, and insight. During my summer breaks I attend bible study at my parish. At other times I rely on books, videos, and anointed friendships that help me to continue to grow in the Word. I consider myself an enlightened novice of the Word! The more I learn the more I want to learn. I truly cannot get enough. My hunger for knowing and understanding God often seems insatiable. My need to apply His Word in my life is tremendous.

> *Your word, Lord, stands forever; it is firm as the heavens. Through all generations your truth endures; fixed to stand firm like the earth. By your edicts they stand firm to this day, for all things are your servants. Had your teaching not been my delight, I would have perished in my affliction. I will never forget your precepts; through them you give me life. I am yours; save me, for I cherish your precepts. The wicked hope to destroy me, but I pay heed to your decrees. I have seen the limits of all perfection, but your command is without bounds.*
> *Psalm 119:89-96*

> *Happy those who do not follow the counsel of the wicked, Nor go the way of sinners, nor sit in company with scoffers. Rather, the law of the Lord is their joy; God's law they study day and night.*
> *Psalm 1:1–3*

This book is the natural culmination of many events and revelations over the past five years. It truly comes out of my desire to share the Word in a valuable way for today's parents. The belief behind this book is that the main goal of parents is to raise children to

> My son, keep my words, and treasure my commands.
>
> *Proverbs 7:1*

and for God. Raising your children to God necessitates turning to His Word. Raising your children for God necessitates turning to His Word as well. The amazing thing (well, one of them) about God's Word is the peace and well-being that is found within. Peace and well-being that is intended to be a part of our life everyday. We shouldn't let another day go by without using the Word of God as the guiding force in raising our family.

Priorities

I believe there is a strong presence that we, as parents, struggle against in raising our children. Many of us are trying our best to raise faith-filled children in a very secular world. We are attempting to "do the right thing" for our children but in the process are making many mistakes. These mistakes arise from that struggle. I see examples of these every day in my classroom. I hear them every day in conversations with concerned parents. I live them in my own house with my three sons. We have let many of our priorities be set by the society we live in and in doing so have set the wrong priorities. Our true priorities have been set for thousands of years. Unlike today's priorities, God's priorities have never changed. Raising children based upon God's priorities means the same yesterday, today, and tomorrow. God looks for our children to put Him first in life and promises then that our lives will be filled with His blessings.

The great struggle that we currently face exists because we are attempting to raise the children God gave us in the secular world where He put us! We often find that there is a vast chasm between what is right and what just "is." As parents we find ourselves in the middle of the struggle between God's way and the secular way. God's way, which never changes, and the secular way, which constantly changes. When we continue to follow a path that is not based upon the Truth, as found in scripture, we are jeopardizing our children's earthly lives and, more importantly, our children's eternal lives. Quite frankly, we are responsible for them in a way that might very well be beyond our comprehension. We spend time worrying about their physical well-being and their academic successes but spend comparatively little time devoted to their spiritual well-being. However, based upon scripture, it is clear that setting our priorities straight with God will open an enormous amount of blessings for our children's earthly lives.

Just because we struggle as parents doesn't indicate that we are bad parents. We are simply parents in need of wisdom, guidance and support. Consider how willing we are to turn to figures we believe to be authoritative. We are looking for guidance and are willing to accept it in whatever way it appears, regardless of the consequences. We cannot continue to allow the secular way to win out because it is easier for us and more accepted in society. Our goal as parents is not to satisfy ourselves, our friends and neighbors, or our children. Our goal as parents is to satisfy God with the job he has put before us. For me, The Parable of the Talents (coins or money), found in Matthew 25:14–30, is a reminder of the great responsibility we have with our children. In this scripture verse

I, the Lord, am your God, who brought you out of the land of Egypt, that place of slavery. You shall not have other gods besides me. You shall not carve idols for yourselves in the shape of anything in the sky above or on the earth below or in the waters beneath the earth; you shall not bow down before them or worship them. For I, the Lord, your God, am a jealous God, inflicting punishment for their fathers' wickedness on the children of those who hate me, down to the third and fourth generation; but bestowing mercy down to the thousandth generation, on the children of those who love me and keep my commandments.

Exodus 20:2–6

we are told about three different servants. Each servant is given some coins. These servants are expected to do something worthwhile with these coins. The story goes on to say that the master goes away but will return (just like ours). We then find out what each servant did with the coins. The first doubles his in value, and likewise the second, but the third buries his, in essence, accomplishing nothing. When the master returns and each servant gives an accounting of what he has done (just like we will) the master is furious with the third servant who, out of fear, did nothing. The master then tells another servant, *"And throw this useless servant into the darkness outside, where there will be wailing and grinding of teeth." Matthew 25:30* This is a powerful message of expectation. I believe it is especially relevant to our role as parents. God expects much from us and we don't want to let Him down.

I set before you here, this day, a blessing and a curse; a blessing for obeying the commandments of the Lord, your God, which I enjoin on you today; a curse if you do not obey the commandments of the Lord, your God, but turn aside from the way I ordain for you today, to follow other gods, whom you have not known.
Deuteronomy 11:26–28

Lovers of your teaching have much peace; for them there is no stumbling block.
Psalm 119:165

So, like the servants that were given talents and expected to do something worthwhile to increase their value, we are expected to do something worthwhile with our children. This also means that we should nurture our children in a way that they take responsibility for their lives and their actions. We want our children to learn that they, too, must be useful, productive adults living for God. No matter where we look, scripture repeatedly gives us the same message. Nothing comes before God and everything is for God. It is all about setting priorities. So, our only concern should be in satisfying God, in pleasing and praising God. Everything else will follow. In seeking God's kingdom first, we will automatically do the best for ourselves, our friends and neighbors, and our children. This is God's promise.

Of course this is contrary to the messages our children receive throughout the day. In fact the secular message of competition and working hard for something often seeps into our Christian lives. I found this to be the case when I was lamenting to a dear friend that I didn't know what God "wanted from me." I told her that I was praying often, hard, and sincerely and didn't feel like I was "getting anywhere." She looked at me with eyes filled with love, concern, and surprise. As matter-of-factly as the sun rises each day she responded, "Cheryl, there's nothing you can do for God but accept and return His love." In that brief response I realized that I was working for God's love and graces the same way I was working for a promotion at work. And, of course, there would never be anything I could do to earn or keep God's love. He simply loved me regardless of my sins, faults, and misguided ways. What a revelation! All I needed to do was accept this unconditional love and, of my own free will, return it to Him. Now that's an awesome message we need to make sure our children are receiving day-in and day-out. As often as we tell them they need to make good decisions or brush their teeth we also need to be telling them of God's unconditional love and commitment to their earthy well-being and eternal salvation. This, in and of itself, will help them forge a personal relationship with God that will transcend their earthly woes and misfortune. Who wouldn't love some great and powerful being that only wants the very best for us? It doesn't get better than that.

> *But seek first the kingdom of God and his righteousness, and all these things will be given you besides.*
> *Matthew 7:33*

For the sake of our children, and our families, it is time to set our priorities according to scripture. Indeed, for us to make a difference in the world, we must make a difference in our family. Our contribution is our children. Teaching our children to love and be in fellowship with God will ensure that our contribution will be the best it can be.

This may seem like a daunting task but remember that God gives us enough manna for each and every day (Exodus 16:4). He gives us everything we need to navigate the waterways of our life, nothing more and nothing less. In fact, it makes perfect sense that God's kingdom starts within our family. We are living in a secular world that is filled with opportunities to choose God, to represent God, and to please God. God continuously looks to us to see that we are choosing Him above all else. He would like to know that we recognize His hand in our lives. When we praise Him, give Him gratitude, and love Him we are in union with Him. He does not need our praise, love, and glory. It helps us in our lives with Him and not the other way around. Once we have done that, we have established for our families all the graces and blessings that will allow us to continue to walk with God. God will be with us uphill and downhill, through hills and valleys, over streams and through deserts. A walk with God is the most amazing experience we will ever have.

Of course the opposite is true as well. We are living in a secular world that is filled with opportunities to deny God, to turn away from God, and to displease God. What we choose to do is, as always, up to us. Where do we put our time and money? How do we conduct our daily life? What kinds of friendships have we forged? All these answers will give us a clear picture of our priorities and the priorities we are establishing for our children. In my household, summertime seems to translate to computer time for my children. I understand (that's the compassion part) their need to take a complete break from school and all the demands of the school year. I also understand (here's the authority part) that how I allow them to spend their time is what I teach them to value. So, (here's the balance) I make them earn their computer time through prayer, reading, and other activities. My message to them says, "I understand your need and enjoyment of playing computer games BUT I believe that time with God is more important." It's a message that I guarantee they understand.

Having said that, I believe that it is never too late to bring our children in line with the teachings found in scripture. It is never too late to use scripture as the guiding force in raising our family, tending to our marriage, and blessing our lives. Being rooted in our faith allows God to bring into our life all the blessings that he has in store for us: people, events, and opportunities. Putting God first allows our lives to grow in wonderful ways.

There are so many "earthly" benefits from choosing God. You've heard the saying, "No God, No Peace; Know God, Know Peace." There truly is an incredible sense of peace and well-being that comes from a life based upon God's priorities. Helping our children put God first gives them great freedom and strength as well. Scripture helps us prioritize our secular existence and show God that we understand that our treasure is with Him. Raising a child steeped in this awareness creates a young person able to withstand the difficulties that come with growing up. A child enveloped in the love and salvation of Jesus will grow into a fine, upstanding, moral, success-ful adult. With God, our children become great contributors to the common good of our society. They become compassionate leaders, responsible parents, diligent workers, and moral neighbors. I firmly believe that if we raise our children to understand their innate place with God we will be raising children with less inclination for anxiety, greed, avarice, addictions, depressions, envy, and an ever-expanding list of ailments that plague our society. We are giving our children the most important piece of their life's puzzle when we give them a relationship with God. Committing ourselves, and our children, to God's way is the most valuable and worthwhile commitment we will ever make.

> Honor the Lord with your wealth, with the first fruits of all your produce, Then will your barns be filled with grain, with new wine your vats will overflow.
> Proverbs 3:9

24

The Value of Prayer

Last summer my two youngest sons and I took a week long trip to visit my father in Oregon. There is a beautiful grotto there that I like to visit whenever I'm in Oregon. This time, because I was with my children, we also visited the gift shop. I have to say that I am not opposed to capitalism and certainly understand that even grottos have bills to pay. Quite frankly, there were many things I would have purchased had my budget allowed. Nonetheless, my 12-year old son was on a mission to find a pen. All of our sightseeing trips ended with a pen purchase, which I thought was a neat way to capture the day. Anyhow, he found a pen and brought it to me. In big letters it said *GAP (God Answers Prayers)*. I like that he picked that particular pen and he knew he had me with that one. He knew I would go along with that purchase without a

> *I tell you, if he does not get up to give him the loaves because of their friendship, he will get up to give him whatever he needs because of his persistence.*
> *Luke 11:5–8*
>
> *And Jesus said to the centurion, "You may go; as you have believed, let it be done for you."*
> *Matthew 8:13*

hitch. My son knows that I firmly believe that God does, in fact, answer prayers.

When you live your life with and for God you can be assured that your prayers are heard. And, of course, there's that understanding that sometimes the answer is "No." Nonetheless, God answers prayers. Remember there's also that understanding that we should be careful of what we pray for because we might get it! Our world is filled with these axioms. They are testaments to the fact that God answers prayers. Scripture, too, is filled with this fact. There are many people who cite examples in scripture of God answering prayers. Sometimes, as we read in the book of Daniel, the answers are immediate. Other times they come when our "receptors" are clear and open. Regardless, throughout the bible we are reminded of God's faithfulness to his people. As baptized followers of Christ, we lay claim to the great blessing of that faithfulness. The bible, especially the Gospels, is filled with examples, illustrations, stories, and parables about praying, praying persistently, and praying with faith. Teaching our children the value of prayer is the most priceless lesson we can teach. When we teach our children to turn to God we have given them a lifelong blessing. Jesus gave us invaluable examples of prayer. We learn from Him the need for quiet, meditative prayer and the need for open, honest prayer. When I meditate on Jesus' prayer in the garden of Gethsemane I am reminded that I can offer up my "ideas" to God but it is best if I let Him call the final shots. My confidence is in His omnipotence and omniscience and not my needs, wants, or perspective of things. He can, afterall, see the big picture and I find great peace in that. It is what we want to share with our children; A simple but true understanding that God really does know best.

We live on a small court in a small neighborhood. Given the size of the neighborhood and the limited number of children, my youngest son has never had anyone his own age to play with. Anyhow, a house went up for sale a few doors away from us and I suggested we pray that a friend would move in. It is my firm belief that one of God's great anointings comes in the form of friendships. My life has been richly blessed by the friends that God has graciously given me. So, it made sense to turn to Him for help. It certainly seemed like this would be in line with His will. Remember that God, being omniscient, already knows what we need but allows us to use our free will to ask Him to enter our lives and fill those needs. He would never break His own rules and just barge in. When I teach my middle school students about developing a relationship with God I use the illustration that He is at the front door. I have the students imagine the door unlocked with God on the outside. I tell them that even though the door is unlocked He won't open it on His own. He will wait till they turn the knob and let Him in. So, after a few days of turning to God for a neighborhood friend, my son did indeed meet someone. Unbeknownst to us, while we were praying for a friend to move into the house a couple of doors away, a new family moved into a house in the back of the neighborhood. It just so happened that they had a son who was my son's age! The boys have since forged a wonderful relationship. And I am, once again, reminded that God does indeed answer our prayers. What continues to reveal itself to me is God's willingness to work out the details when we let Him. A home for sale prompted us to invite God to answer our prayer for a friend. We left the rest up to Him.

> *The king was overjoyed and gave orders to lift Daniel out of the den. And when Daniel was lifted from the den, no wound was found on him, because he had trusted in his God.*
> Daniel 6:23

There are many ways to acknowledge the importance of prayer in our homes. There is a reason that morning, evening, and meal-time prayers are so wonderful. Morning prayer is a beautiful time to thank God for the night's sleep, ask Him to manifest his blessings in our day, and to offer our day (whatever it may hold) to Him for His Glory. Evening prayer again offers a time to show thanksgiving for the day and everything it held (good and not-so-good!) and ask God to stay with us through the night. Of course, throughout the day it is also good to keep God on our mind. We can be an example of this through little statements we make, "I know God will be with us when we take our trip to see grandpa," or "I am so thankful to God that my cold only lasted a couple of days." When someone sneezes I make a point of saying, "God bless you," not just, "Bless you." Whenever possible we need to bring God into our life and the lives of our children. Simple but bold sentences are the easiest way to do just that. We don't have to be "over-the-top" in our zeal but simply state the facts, "God sure blessed you with that great job." Or, "God is clearly smiling on you today!"

Food and its preparation are blessings from God and should be recognized as such. Mealtime, in and of itself, is also an occasion for special prayers. So much of our faith resides in the fact that Jesus gave himself to us at the Last Supper. All meals should, in some way, give gratitude to God. I used to dread the grocery store. It always felt like such an infringement on my time. Then, a few years ago, I realized that grocery shopping is a blessing and now, every time I shop, I thank God for the ability to buy groceries and feed my family. However we do it, we should make sure that we teach our children that prayer has many forms (gratitude, petition, worship) and that the entire day is filled with opportunities to talk with God.

> And Jesus said to the centurion, "You may go; as you have believed, let it be done for you."
>
> Matthew 8:13

If this is new to you and your family, be prepared for negative reactions! But don't let this hinder you, consider it a God given opportunity to get into the trenches and do God's work in your family. Wherever you are in your prayer life, keep persevering while you work God into a bigger part of your family life. Be persistent in your endeavor to bring prayer and a living relationship with God into your children's lives. Prayer for and with our children should be our foundation as parents.

My biggest rewards as a mother have been when my children ask me to pray with them or for them. Quite frankly, it is easy to question ourselves as parents. To make matters worse there aren't many accolades that come with parenting, especially during the pre-teen and teenage years. Consequently, when something happens to affirm our job, we need to grab it with gusto! This is how I reacted when my 7th grader asked me to pray with him for a special request. He wanted to pray that his teacher would accept a late paper. This was quite momentous for me. I have to say that it didn't matter to me one bit that my son had a late paper. Nothing could replace my joy in the fact that he asked me to pray with him. From my perspective (and I think this is very valuable to share with you) my son's lost paper was actually a blessing. A few years ago I would have reprimanded him for losing track of his work. I would not have recognized the opportunity God gave me to share a prayer with my son. My focus would have been purely academic. However, at this point in my life I just felt joyful for the opportunity to practice what I preach! It is amazing how God, in all His wisdom, continues to shower us with great and wonderful blessings. Sadly, we often mistake them or don't recognize them as such. God is doing His best to work with us.

Anyhow, for me this wasn't about God answering or not answering my son's prayer regarding his late work.

> He said to her, "Daughter, your faith has saved you. Go in peace and be cured of your affliction."
> *Mark 5:34*

> I was still occupied with my prayers, confessing my sin and the sin of my people Israel, presenting my petition to the Lord, my God, on behalf of his holy mountain I was still occupied with this prayer, when Gabriel, the one whom I had seen before in vision, came to me in rapid flight at the time of the evening sacrifice. He instructed me in these words: "Daniel, I have now come to give you understanding. When you began your petition, an answer was given which I have come to announce, because you are beloved . . .
> *Daniel 9:20-23*

This was actually God answering my prayer. A prayer asking for help in bringing my children to Him. This was really all about God giving my son and I an opportunity to connect for a very special moment. (For those of you who are interested, my son's teacher did not accept his late paper.) Fortunately, I saw the moment for what it was, a glorious way to raise my son up to God. On the other hand, my son might have assumed that God either didn't answer his prayer or that God answered but the answer was "No." I, however, was able to see the "bigger picture" and understood that it wasn't about my son's prayer. It was about my prayer and my prayer was answered with a resounding, "YES, I can do that. I can help you bring your children to Me!"

Indeed, seeing things in a new way has allowed me to see God's hand in many situations. Once we are able to see God's graces in our life, we really do begin to see them everywhere! God's graces are just waiting to be embraced. If we are able to start to look at our life with our children in this light we will be awed at all the wonderful things God is doing for us right now. Helping our children see the graces flowing in their lives will help them forge a life of great joy and peace.

Bringing prayer into our children's lives has another dimension as well. Besides teaching our children the great joy of praying it is also a grace to be able to pray for our children. I consider us, as parents, quite blessed that something so powerful can be so easy. This is something we can do at anytime during the day or night. We can pray for them while we are waiting in line at the grocery store, while we are cooking dinner, or driving to work. You name the place and we can be there praying! When we hug our children we should invite God into the relationship with a simple, "Stay with us forever, Lord." It can be said out loud or in our heart. When we tuck our children in bed at night we should remember to thank their guardian angels for the day spent by their side. Always, and in every way, we should pray for our children. Pray persistently and with confidence in the Lord, our God.

Finally, I think it is important for us to pray for all the people in our children's lives: friends, teachers, neighbors, and coaches. I believe this creates a prayerful atmosphere in which our children can exist. Prayer is the ultimate win-win situation! Enjoy the rewards.

First of all, then, I ask that supplications, prayers, petitions, and thanksgivings be offered for everyone, for kings and for all authority that we may lead a quiet and tranquil life in all devotion and dignity. This is good and pleasing to God our savior, who wills everyone to be saved and to come to knowledge of the truth.

1 Timothy 2:1–4

Bless Your Children

Of all the stories in the bible, one of the most intriguing is the story of Jacob stealing Esau's blessing from Isaac (Genesis 27:1–45). Ultimately the story is about the immense value of parental blessings. What mother doesn't want her children to be richly blessed? What father wouldn't want to bestow great blessings upon his children? Clearly, blessings are the most valuable gift we give our children.

Fortunately, we are able to do that for all our children. Not just one, not just our first born, but all our children are able to receive our blessings. The bible tells us if we, through our faith, are children of God in Christ, then we are heirs to the promises made to Abraham. That is incredibly powerful because the blessings that God gave

> I will make of you a great nation, and I will bless you; I will make your name great, so that you will be a blessing. I will bless those who bless you and curse those who curse you. All the communities of the earth shall find blessing in you.
>
> *Genesis 12:2–3*
>
> Blessings are for the head of the just, but a rod for the back of the fool.
>
> *Proverbs 10:6*

33

Abraham were powerful. Remember that God said He would bless everyone who blessed Abraham and He would curse everyone who cursed Abraham (Genesis 12:3). This reveals to me two very powerful messages. First, thousands of years ago God was saying that he was listening to people's blessings and curses. He was giving us a fair warning about the power of our words. This scripture verse tells me that God spoke the world into being and, likewise, puts great emphasis on the way we use our words as well.

In addition to that God is saying that He would be acting upon the words we utter, in essence telling us we will reap what we sow. Sometimes I can overhear the exchanges that take place between my children. I might be in the kitchen and they are in the front room watching television. An argument might erupt regarding the show or some other silly thing. I listen and determine if intervention is needed. Over the years I have become quite skilled at stopping myself from jumping into the middle of all their tiffs. My wisdom and understanding have grown as a parent. God, the ultimate source of wisdom and understanding, is also listening to our exchanges, our tiffs, and our utterances. In one forceful passage God is revealing to us the power of the spoken word. He is reminding us of the strength of the spoken word. He is saying that every word has power.

This passage has another revelation that is just as stalwart. It is telling us that we are heirs to the promises made to Abraham. Through our faith, our children have inherited these promises as well. God's blessings are our blessings AND are our blessings to give. This is quite an inheritance! Can you imagine a great, great, great uncle leaving you a million dollars and you not claiming it? Just leaving it in the estate. Of course you wouldn't, so why not claim this great blessing we have as descendents of Abraham? I urge you to lay claim to it today and make it an integral part of raising your children.

As you can see, learning and understanding the history of our faith is amazing. As I mentioned earlier, when we consider the power of God's promise to Abraham we are actually learning the power of the spoken word. We are learning that our words will have a powerful impact on our lives and the lives of our children. Blessings are all about the strength and power held in the spoken word.

So, whether we look at Rachel "stealing" Isaac's blessing for Jacob or Jesus becoming the Word Incarnate (the Word made flesh), we see the magnitude of the spoken word in our faith history. We learn that the words we use with and for our children and the blessings we bestow upon them are immensely powerful.

Clearly, blessings should be an important part of raising our children.

> *The trustworthy man will be richly blessed; he who is in haste to grow rich will not go unpunished.*
> *Proverbs 28:20*
>
> *May God give to you of the dew of the heavens and of the fertility of the earth abundance of grain and wine. Let peoples serve you, and nations pay you homage; be master of your brothers, and may your mother's sons bow down to you. Cursed be those who curse you, and blessed be those who bless you.*
> *Genesis 27:28-29*

Blessings can be for everything and anything. Blessings are actually quite different from prayers. Prayers are our dialogue with our Creator. They may be gratitude, petition, meditative, or worship. On the other hand, blessings stem from our God-given authority. Blessings are those beautiful words we bestow on our children as they leave for the movies or go to school, "May your guardian angel watch over you and guard you," or, "May all your words and actions be pleasing to God today." Blessings allow us to use our influence to bring graces into our children's lives. God's grace is what allows us to share in God's life. This is one of God's precious gifts to us.

Up until a couple of years ago, I quite consistently withheld blessings from my children. I guess it never occurred to me that I could and should bless my children. Worse still, I actually cursed my children with such phrases as, "I hope someday you have children that are this disrespectful to you!" or, "I hope your children argue with you all day long!" or, "I hope your kids never listen to you and you'll know what your dad and I go through!" You get the picture.

Then, one day, the Holy Spirit quite literally opened my eyes. To my great dismay I realized that as long as I continued to put these curses into my children's lives, they were sure to come true. And why, in Heaven's name, would I want my children to experience these harsh sentences? Why would I, the mother, want anything other than the absolute best, most awesome life possible for my children. And, quite frankly, isn't that what my eternal Father wants for me as well? So, my words and thoughts took a quick, wide, drastic U-turn. Cursing my children was just bringing a curse into my own family. I was stunned that I could have been so careless with my words.

> I said that I would never break my covenant with you, but that you were not to make a pact with the inhabitants of this land, and you were to pull down their altars. Yet you have not obeyed me. What did you mean by this? For now I tell you, I will not clear them out of your way; they shall oppose you and their gods shall become a snare for you.
> Judges 2:2–3

> And if you belong to Christ, then you are Abraham's descendant, heirs according to the promise.
> Galatians 3:29

Now my days are filled with loving words and thoughts to help my children on their journey. This doesn't mean I don't get frustrated with my kids. I certainly do, but I have learned to be more cautious with the words that I use in my frustration. My frustration has also helped me grow as a parent. I see these years as an opportunity to grow into all God would like me to become. Again I reiterate that this doesn't mean my home is in a state of constant bliss. That would be heaven and heaven is yet to come. However, I now truly understand the words "unconditional love." I also have a new level of patience (even if it still is not high enough!) and compassion that I never had before. So, regardless of how frustrated I am with my children, I am quite committed to blessing them in every way possible. I am forever grateful for their guardian angels, the Holy Spirit, and their salvation. These blessings are added to the prayers of gratitude and confidence that the Lord will bring people, events, and opportunities into their lives that have His anointing.

Like prayer, blessings are something that extend beyond my children as well. I want God's anointing in all of the lives of my students, my friends, my children's friends, family, neighbors, teachers and so on. My days are filled with thoughts of blessings for people I pass on the street, at work, or in the store. I believe that we have a great ability to care for others in a very real way through our prayers and blessings. Blessings, like love, are greater when given away.

Responsibility

I once read that compassion without wisdom was an unbalanced answer to today's ills. I felt the words made sense. They reminded me very much of the words, "Give a man fish and he eats for a day. Teach a man to fish and he eats for a lifetime." Clearly compassion is very needed in our ailing society. However, the key is to be compassionate while being wise. In other words, allow your heart to comfort and embrace while allowing your intellect to find and offer solutions. God gave us both heart and intellect and expects us to use both.

Those words about compassion were so profound to me that I shared them with our principal. They seemed appropriate because we were in the middle of yet another parent-student-school situation. Once again we were torn, deciding the right course of ac-

Therefore all you have brought upon us, all you have done to us, you have done by a proper judgment.

Daniel 3:31

Chastised a little, they shall be greatly blessed, because God tried them and found them worthy of himself.

Wisdom 4:5

tion for a particularly difficult student. Do we, as a private Christian school, avoid consequences or do we apply consequences? Do we make the student accept responsibility or do we allow the student to walk away from any responsibility? It was as if we were always in the middle of this dilemma. We were cautious to be judgmental (lest we be judged) and yet knew we needed to make a judgment (because that is how our students will learn). Needless to say, making this difficult decision even more difficult were the parents. Like many parents today, these parents were pushing for no consequences. They felt other people and circumstances were to blame. They were appealing to our sense of, "Jesus said whoever is without sin should cast the first stone," dilemma. They, in all honesty, wanted to find fault with anyone, and everyone, except their own child.

Being the mother of three boys, and having been on the receiving end of this situation, I understood their need to protect and defend their child. It is, by and large, a fairly common reaction. But I have come to realize how important it is **not** to always take this stand. For the sake of the child, it is by far better for him or her to take responsibility and believe that the consequences are fair. The critical part of this is actually helping a child see consequences as fair (even if the parent thinks they aren't!). As difficult as this often is, authority figures in a child's life should have the respect and honor due the position (Romans 13:7). As a

> *The honesty of the upright guides them; the faithless are ruined by their duplicity.*
> *Proverbs 11:3*
>
> *He who listens to salutary reproof will abide among the wise. He who rejects admonition despises his own souls, but he who heeds reproof gains understanding.*
> *Proverbs 15:31–32*
>
> *My sons, do not disdain the discipline of the Lord or lose heart when reproved by Him; for whom the Lord loves, he disciplines,; he scourges every son he acknowledges.*
> *Hebrews 12:5–6*
>
> *A path to life is his who heeds admonition, but he who disregards reproof goes astray.*
> *Proverbs 10:17*

whole, we have moved away from this and yet scripture tells us it is so. Scripture clearly says that people in positions of authority should receive our honor and respect. I was bothered once when I heard a parent tell a person in authority that she would have her son comply with a particular rule when she (the parent) saw other children abiding by it as well. This parent was saying, first of all, that the person in authority had no authority. This parent was actually telling this person that his/her authority had no weight as far as she was concerned. Second of all, this parent blatantly said she would not require her son to follow the rule until other students were under compliance. This would be like telling a police officer that was handing you a speeding ticket, "I'll stop speeding when everyone else does." Hopefully we wouldn't think of saying something like that, even if we might think it and even if it were true. We have to teach our children to be respectful in the same way. It goes completely against scripture when we are disrespectful to someone in authority. Obviously this doesn't cover all the possible scenarios of people abusing authority but nonetheless does require of us a greater understanding of our responsibility to teach our children to respect people in particular positions. Scripture tells us that only a fool disregards discipline. This is how we learn and this is how our children learn. When we take that tool away we are diminishing our children's opportunities to learn and grow as God intended. It is quite a daunting task to raise my children and I want all the help I can get!

A great scriptural example of embracing consequences is in the book of Daniel. We see that Shadrach, Meshach, and Agednego, after being cast into a white-hot furnace, are praising the Lord! They are taking full responsibility for their actions and praising God as well. They had made a bad decision about their actions and now were believing the consequences to be fair and just. I find that heroic and it inspires me. Meditating on these words makes me realize how important responsibility really is in our children's lives.

This is something that is seen again and again in the bible. We should be encouraging our children to take responsibility for themselves and their actions. And in a thankful way! We can look at consequences as a way to make things right (the bible is filled with the need for penance) and stay on the path to God. Looking at things from this perspective we can see how, even in a white-hot furnace, Shadrach, Meshach, and Agednego are praising God. Could we say the same for ourselves? Is this what we teach our children?

> He who loves correction loves knowledge, but he who hates reproof is stupid.
> *Proverbs 12:1*

According to scripture, this is exactly what we should be teaching our children. Consider all the recent scandals our nation has experienced. Not only do we see countless people avoiding responsibility, we then see them avoiding consequences as well. This couldn't be further from what scripture dictates. When we consider that our earthly existence is just like a "mist," then helping our children get it right should be of the utmost importance to us. We all make mistakes and should learn from them.

My own children are at an age where I enjoy challenging them in intellectual or spiritual ways. I can't say that they enjoy it, but I sure do. A few days ago my son did not want to help unload the groceries from the van. He was glued to the television and was eating something that was nice and cold. He told me he couldn't help me because his blueberries would get mushy (in the 1 1/2 minutes it takes to unload the van). I asked him how he would defend that decision when he stood before God, "Well, gee, how could I help my mom? My blueberries would get mushy." Could he picture himself saying that? What would God's reaction be? It seems like such a small incident but I really wanted him to imagine himself before God. If my son really felt that my request was unreasonable then he has to know that I, too, have to justify myself before the Lord. We are all responsible for our own decisions, our own lives. As parents we are also responsible for raising our children in a way that they can be held accountable for themselves. God has given us these children to ultimately bring to Him. So, I feel that the best thing we can do is to encourage our children to live lives that are truly justifiable to our Lord. Fortunate or not, children learn accountability through consequences. Have you ever noticed that when we fail to learn a particular lesson God will, in His grace and mercy, continue to give us opportunities to learn until we get it right? Why not let our children learn this at a much earlier age than we did? Of course no one is perfect, but trying to give our children a sense of purpose to guide their lives is very important. They should have an ultimate goal: Heaven. Then, when we justify ourselves before the Lord, we, too, will have half a chance! Ultimately, teaching children the great value of personal responsibility gives them a true opportunity to have a life filled with God's graces.

Value Everyone

I have a friend who has the best party options for her children. They can either invite everyone from their class (in the case of her middle school child this means the homeroom class) or they can choose one friend to celebrate with. She simply will not allow her children to be the cause of sadness or angst among kids. And she doesn't throw big, expensive, lavish parties. One of the shindigs in which everyone was invited included such classics as hot dogs, chips, and flash light tag. She and her husband were right there in the mix of things and everyone who came had a great time. I feel blessed to know this woman. She inspires me to live the Word with my family.

Jesus tells us through the Gospels that we should include everyone. Plain and simple. He says to invite the uninvitable, and when attending a party, seat ourselves in the least desirable spot. Who knew the bible had party instructions! Yet, as I said earlier, God wouldn't leave us without details for the care and upbringing of His children. Following His instructions allows our children to be truly rewarded. He tells us that when we spend time with our inner circle of friends, we already have our rewards. Our rewards are their precious and blessed friendships. But, when we decide to include people whom we don't consider part of our circle of friends, then our rewards will be found in heaven. This is a very valuable lesson to teach our children. There are earthly rewards and there are heavenly rewards. When our children do not extend themselves beyond their comfort group, their friends, and their allies, then they do not move into heavenly rewards. As Jesus says, they have already had their recompense. Of course, we can walk a fine line when we begin looking at motive or intention. We certainly don't want to teach our children to "invite the uninvitable" so that they can go to heaven. Instead, we want to teach our children to compassionately reach out to those in need of friends and fellowship. No strings attached. No ulterior motives. Essentially we are teaching our children to do the right thing just for the sake of it.

> *For by the grace given to me I tell everyone among you not to think of himself more highly than one ought to think, but to think soberly, each according to the measure of faith that God has apportioned. For as in one body we have many parts, and all the parts do not have the same function, so we, though many, are one body in Christ and individually parts of one another. Since we have gifts that differ according to the grace given to us, let us exercise them.*
>
> *Romans 12:3–6*

This isn't to suggest that earthly rewards are not a wonderful part of life. They absolutely are. However, when our children learn to solely satisfy their earthly existence, to satiate their carnal wants, then they begin to neglect their spiritual needs. This becomes compounded through adolescence and into young adulthood. Before long we have adults riddled with neurosis, envy, greed, and depression. I believe this is because abso-

> *Rather, when you hold a banquet, invite the poor, the crippled, the lame, the blind; blessed indeed will you be because of their inability to repay you. For you will be repaid at the resurrection of the righteous.*
>
> *Luke 14:13–14*

lutely nothing that we can attain on this earth, in the form of material things, will satisfy the longing we have for God in our heart. Yes, we want to raise our children to have a healthy interest in their physical world. Yes, our children will compete for college acceptances and career opportunities. However, none of their worldly existence should take priority over their eternal salvation. When we teach our children that they are spiritual beings, first and foremost, they will know how to fill the hunger in their soul. And there is a hunger in their soul. God put that hunger there so that they would search Him out. Unless we make sure our children are on the right path, they will assume that things and possessions can quench that desire. When, in fact, nothing can quench that desire but God. Having done our job right, their earthly goals will simply be the icing on the cake. We will have avoided creating individuals who spend a lifetime pursuing one goal after another finding only fleeting satisfaction in the material goods of this world.

One of the most insidious by-products of pursuing temporal goals is the way in which our children treat one another. They learn from so many sources that winning, and being a winner, is the most important part of life. Couple that with their need to fit in with certain groups or peers and we have children filled with angst and stress carelessly mistreating one another. Our children are trying to get by in a culture functioning in direct opposition to the Golden Rule. The Golden Rule, as it is often called, tells us that we should treat others as we would have them treat us. This is firmly rooted in scripture. However, instead of valuing themselves and others, our children are inundated with messages that they are not all they could be unless they have the right shoes, bike, clothes, or electronics. They are also buying into the frenzied idea that there is a limited amount of success "out there" for them to achieve and if they aren't cutthroat enough, they won't get any. How absurd. God's graces are endless, once again, we only need to place our children on the right path.

To begin with we should help our children recognize their own uniqueness as children of God. We should help them recognize their innate value as children of God. In fact, according to scripture, we are intended to work together to make the whole body of Christ. Each of us in his own unique and valuable way. Everyone arrived here with gifts and talents from God that He expects us to use, develop, and share. Our children must **repeatedly** (lets' say as often as they receive the messages to the contrary) receive the message that they are an integral part of God's plan for this world. No one is more or less valuable than another.

> *Only, everyone should live as the Lord as assigned, just as God called each one.*
> *1 Corinthians 7:17*

Some of my most inspirational middle school students are ones who are not part of any particular crowd but are able to fit in with most everyone. These students are able to move from one group of kids to another. They are students who add to whatever mix of peers they are in without sacrificing their own uniqueness. What I see as the common denominator among these kids is that there is no common denominator. Instead, what I notice about these students is that each one is very much his or her own person. They don't lose their personality in a group setting. What I take from this is a firm commitment to teach my children to value themselves and others. I want them to understand Psalm 139 in which we are told that each and every one of us was formed, with great love, by God. We were formed by a God who knows and loves us intimately. In teaching our children to value everyone they encounter we are truly teaching them to value God's work.

> *But I say to you, love your enemies, and pray for those who persecute you, that you may be children of your heavenly Father, for he makes his sun rise on the bad and the good, and causes rain to fall on the just and the unjust. For if you love those who love you, what recompense will you have?*
> *Matthew 5:44–46*

Consequently, I believe there are three distinct aspects of learning to value all people. The first is in teaching our children to value themselves as a critical part of the whole body of Christ. What this really means is that we should always encourage children to see themselves as created by God with certain talents, gifts, and a given nature. While our task as a parent is to encourage and nurture these talents and gifts, it is important to acknowledge that they may be different gifts than we would like to see. My children display characteristics that I, too, have had to come to terms with. One child is fearless, inquisitive, stubborn, and incredibly goal oriented. Another is quite laid back when it comes to setting goals and yet immensely intelligent. Another child is deep, emotional, loving, and easily offended. Understanding that my job is to nurture these young men to be children of God and not necessarily be a pilot, a heart surgeon, and an engineer has really lightened my load! This doesn't mean that I still don't hound them about homework or picking up their room. And there are still all the typical mother-son issues, but my heart understands their existence on a much more spiritual level than ever before. I have come to see them as they are in God's eyes and understand that God's plan for them might be very different than my plans for them. Comforting to me is the new understanding that however different God's plan is for them, it is far superior than anything I could come up with! And if I cooperate with God in raising my children, they truly will be all He has intended for them to be.

I now understand that my ultimate job is to prepare them for a life pleasing to God. In fact, one day it occurred to me that if I continue to try to drastically change my children I am, in effect, telling God His plans aren't up to par! I'm saying that I could make a better call on what should be in store for my children. This is an absurd presumption. So, I have learned to navigate my children's lives in a way that brings them to fruition for God and not for me. By embracing children's uniqueness we are teaching them to embrace their uniqueness as well. I have seen, first hand, what happens when a parent is unwilling, or unable, to accept children with their own dreams, inclinations, and shortcomings. These children are living difficult, unhappy lives trying to be something that they are not meant to be. Again, this doesn't mean we give them free reign, but instead, we guide and nurture with wisdom and prayer. Don't we all know a doctor who really wanted to be a carpenter? Or a teacher who wanted to be an actor? This is the difficult and yet exciting part of being a parent. Helping your child discover his or her own special calling is a beautiful endeavor. So, the first step in helping children fit in with one another is teaching them how valuable they truly are.

> *You formed my inmost being; you knit me in my mother's womb. I praise you, so wonderfully you made me; wonderful are your works! My very self you knew; my bones were not hidden from you, when I was being made in secret, fashioned as in the depths of the earth. Your eyes foresaw my actions; in your book all are written down, my days were shaped, before one came to be.*
>
> *Psalm 139:13–16*

The second aspect of valuing everyone is to teach our children the inherent value of all people. The most obvious way to do this is through the encouraging words we use with our children when talking about his or her peers. We should continuously coax our children to be thoughtful, sympathetic, and considerate whenever the opportunity arises at school or in the neighborhood. We need to encourage our children to be brave enough to step forward and invite their less popular peers to sit at the lunch table or to sign a yearbook. Remember that consistency is the key. To soft-sell such an important message would be a real disservice. I always remember that my children hear messages contrary to mine about a hundred times a day. So, for my message to have an impact, it also has to be just as repetitive.

Let's consider all the information we know as adults and help our children assimilate it through our words and actions. For instance, we often hear that bullies are usually kids who have been bullied themselves. When we share this with our child it might eventually help our child see the situation in a different light. We're not asking our children to accept or formulate excuses but to develop empathy for others. We are then encouraging our children to act with wisdom and compassion when dealing with others.

Our children really do need to understand that God made each of us different and each of us is as valuable as the next. Each of us is a necessary part of the body of Christ (Romans 12:3–6) . Like all the various parts of the human body, we all have purposes and roles to fill. We, as parents, need to cultivate this attitude in our children.

Along with our encouraging words our children should also witness us practicing these traits. Remember my friend who doesn't allow her kids to neglect anyone for a birthday party? Her actions speak loud and clear.

> *For by the grace given me I say to every one of you: Do not think of yourself more highly than you ought, but rather think of yourself with sober judgment, in accordance with the measure of faith God has given you . . . We have different gifts, according to the grace given us . . .*
>
> *Romans 12:3,6*

I believe the third and final aspect of valuing others is to teach our children to value the whole body of Christ. When we help our child see the bigger picture, no matter what it is, we are really teaching our child incredible life-long skills. We are saying that things have value in and of themselves. This is an incredible understanding to impart to our children. Working backwards, you might say that if your child doesn't see that the bigger picture has great significance then your child wouldn't be able to see that all the individual pieces are vitally important. Years ago I taught computer classes at a large corporation. Each instructor had a certain number of classes that they became "experts" in. One of my classes was called PC Overview. It was an introduction to personal computers. I taught the basics. My students learned what files were, where to store them and so on. I always knew that my part of the curriculum was very important. If I fell short in my piece of the overall agenda, the students would be ill prepared for the next class taught by another instructor. I had a responsibility to the students and to the other trainers. The real world requires our children to be cognizant of the "bigger picture." This spiritual lesson has a very real-world application.

We want our children to understand that God has created an entire picture where every soul has a purpose. Consequently, for us to bring to fruition God's plan, we must all partake in it with equal vigor and worth. Teaching our children to value themselves, others, and the whole body of Christ is a beautiful way to honor and be an active participant in God's plan.

The Flesh

t. Paul understood, without a doubt, the on-going battle between flesh and spirit. In fact, he gave great praise to God for the "thorn" in his side knowing full well that this would keep him humble. Humility, as you may know, is a trait of the utmost importance for anyone to be of any use to God.

Our children's lives continually provide opportunities to explore the desires of the flesh and teach them to overcome those desires. As you can well imagine, different phases of growing will introduce different temptations with which children will struggle. However, regardless of the struggle, the underlying lesson, *not to let your flesh rule your existence*, will remain the same throughout. Ultimately this lesson will move our children into adulthood ready to abide by a moral code that will be pleasing to God and will provide a multitude of blessings. The earlier they learn to overcome the will of the flesh, the more successful they will be in life.

We know these desires by a variety of names: temptation, peer pressure, addiction. Rightly so, the connotation of each of these labels is negative. Teaching our children to overcome the desires

Raising Christian Children in a Secular World

of the flesh gives them an incredible foundation from which to grow into responsible, trustworthy, moral, peaceful adults. Fulton J. Sheen, in his book, "Peace of Soul" does a wonderful job tying the anxieties and frustrations of an entire generation to the pursuit of worldly desires. Today our children confront desires of the flesh everywhere. There is no longer a particular street to avert, a particular show to avoid, or a particular magazine to boycott. During the blandest of shows we are confronted by offensive commercials. Flipping through a simple magazine we find explicit advertisements. We live in a society more than ready to convince our children of the immorality of morality.

Of all the messages thrown at our children one distinct message stands out. Our children are told to care for no one but themselves. From every avenue imaginable, our children are encouraged to be self-absorbed and

For those who live according to the flesh are concerned with the things of the flesh, but those who live according to the spirit with the things of the spirit. The concern of the flesh is death, but the concern of the spirit is life and peace. For the concern of the flesh is hostility toward God; it does not submit to the law of God, nor can it; and those who are in the flesh cannot please God. But you are not in the flesh; on the contrary, your are in the spirit, if only the Spirit of God dwells in you. Whoever does not have the Spirit of Christ does not belong to him. But if Christ is in you, although the body is dead because of sin, the spirit is alive because of righteousness. If the Spirit of the one who raised Jesus from the dead dwells in you, the one who raised Christ from the dead will give life to your mortal bodies also, through his Spirit that dwells in you. Consequently, brothers, we are not debtors to the flesh, to live according to the flesh. For if you live according to the flesh, you will die, but if by the spirit you put to death the deeds of the body, you will live.
Romans 8:1–13

self-aggrandizing. In every way thinkable our children are told to win-at-all-costs. Ruthlessness is admired while compassion has no place. People group together to vote someone out instead of people grouping together to keep someone in. Everywhere you turn people are discarding and eliminating one another like yesterday's news. It's actually quite tragic. There always has to be a loser, two losers, or dozens of losers. Someone has to lose so that someone else can win. That's the message. However, as we know, it's the wrong message. It's the message that we have to counter at all times. It is a message that fills our children with anxiety and frustration: a false perception of the value of material goods and earthly successes.

In addition to the anxieties and frustrations that such a message creates for our children there is another very serious problem with that message. No one actually has to lose for someone else to win. Think about it . . . if someone had to lose for someone else to win then God would be limited in His blessings, limited in His graces, limited in His power and plan for the world. Nothing could be further from the truth. So, when our children are encouraged to win and have no regard for those who lose, our children are learning to underestimate God's power and overestimate Satan's.

> *What I do, I do not understand. For I do not do what I want, but I do what I hate . . . The willing is ready at hand, but doing the good is not. For I do not do the good I want, but I do the evil I do not want.*
> *Romans 7:15,18-19*

When we study scripture and understand God's plan for our children, we can rest assured that there are no losers in this great plan. Children should be taught that in some ways we all win. Those winnings are different based upon each person and his or her talents and blessings but everyone is a winner in God's plan. Indeed, we find out that when our children help others, they are actually helping themselves. When our children bless others, they are actually blessing themselves. Scripture tells us that there is a common good to strive for. When our children ignore the common good and try to get ahead at the expense of others they are putting unnecessary delays in God's plan for their lives. They are a delight to Satan when they act on their fleshly desires. When our children learn to put their self-interests first, they make it more difficult for their spiritual selves to grow and mature. They push the blessings and graces of God much further out of reach. Sadly, we have been sold a bag of goods and Satan is most certainly delighted. As scripture says, there are seven things that are an abomination to the Lord: haughty eyes, a lying tongue, hands that shed innocent blood, a heart that plots wicked schemes, feet that run swiftly to evil, a false witness who utters lies, and he who sows discord among brothers. Remember that we are all brothers in God's eyes. Let us teach our children that the way of the spirit is mightier than the way of the flesh. Let our children not be an abomination to the Lord.

To begin working with your child in this area, consider some of the things that your child often succumbs to. It might be anger, impatience, gossip, greed, or envy. These traits, then, become the traits that you want to help your child overcome, to not "give in to." For example, many children tend to be procrastinators. If they could have their druthers, they would do all homework on the last night before it's due.

> *For we must all appear before the judgment seat of Christ, so that each one may receive recompense, according to what he did in the body, whether good or evil.*
>
> *2 Corinthians 5:10*

Although many parents feel this is a normal part of growing up, I believe it is our responsibility to help our children overcome this, to not "give in to it." Waiting until the last minute is not a desirable habit. Consider the problems that this trait would pose for adults.

While we are teaching our children to manage time correctly (and not wait until the last minute) we are also teaching our children the trait of self-control and self-management. They are learning to do what is right, which is not necessarily what they "want." They are learning to overcome the selfishness of the flesh (to avoid homework) and pursue a more beneficial avenue. Denial can be a very valuable lesson. This applies to all the controlling, manipulating forces that influence our children. More and more children have come to expect vacations, the latest electronic games and devices, and cars when they are of driving age. As Fulton Sheen points out, what used to be luxuries have become necessities.

We can do a great service for our children when we instill in them, at any age, that only God will fill the longing in their hearts and souls. We certainly have been witness to the fact that multitudes of people, looking for fulfillment in earthly possessions, have ruined and destroyed their own lives, the lives of their loved ones, and countless other innocent victims. This exists on many levels throughout our culture. The idea that winning is everything, together with a real loss of compassion towards fellow human beings, has left our society in a miserable state. Countless people suffer unnecessarily due to their misguided notion of limited blessings in the world. From this false belief has grown a vast number of people trying to grasp at earthly successes, regardless of the human toll. All of this stems from our idea that once our flesh is satiated, we, too, will be satiated. And nothing could be further from the truth. Let us, then, give our children the real knowledge that God will fulfill, God will provide, God will prevail.

> *We know that our old self was crucified with him, so that our sinful body might no longer be in slavery to sin.*
>
> Romans 6:6

The New Temple

My son, a wonderfully talented skateboarder, recently asked me a very interesting question, "Mom, is skateboarding without a helmet a sin? Like if you are doing crazy things and you don't have a helmet on?" So, right away a couple of thoughts rush through my mind. First, what in the world is this kid doing on his skateboard? Second, *is* skateboarding without a helmet a sin?

When a child opens any dialogue that has the word "sin" in it, you immediately invite the Holy Spirit to be a part of the conversation! And that is exactly what I did. I told my son that, although I wasn't sure, I actually felt that I could make a case for skateboarding without a helmet as being a sin. My reasoning? Our body is a temple to the Holy Spirit. Our bodies, as St. Paul tells us in 1 Corinthians, really don't belong to us. They've been purchased, at

> *Do you not know that your body is a temple of the Holy Spirit within you, whom you have from God, and that you are not your own? For you have been purchased at a price. Therefore glorify God in your body.*
> *1 Corinthians 6:19-20*

a high price, by Jesus. So, when we act irresponsibly with our bodies, we are jeopardizing the temple that is God's dwelling place. That certainly can't be a good thing. So, I could see how wild skateboarding, especially without a helmet, could be a sinful thing.

Of course I also slipped in, as nonchalantly as possible, the idea that many other things would be sinful as well. Scripture warns us against immorality, drunkenness, gluttony, and many other sins of the flesh. Teaching our children to value and respect their bodies as a dwelling place of the Holy Spirit is an important part of growing up.

Consider the latest statistics regarding teenage obesity and diabetes. They are quite alarming and we should be taking them very seriously. Teaching our children to value their physical bodies as temples to the Holy Spirit means teaching our children proper eating, exercising, and resting habits. Knowledge is power and when we give our children the knowledge of proper diet, nutrition, and physical safety we are empowering them to care for the temple that God has given them. Of course this also translates into us caring for our own physical health and well-being. In the past five years my children have watched me commit to an exercise routine that includes walking, cycling, and Tai Chi. In addition to my physical commitment to exercising, my children have also seen that my interest in pursuing information regarding health and nutrition has been awakened. This isn't to say that I run a nutritionist's dream kitchen but that my children know the value I place on physical well-being. We are, after all, spiritual beings in physical bodies. If we tend to one part of ourselves at the exclusion of another, we lose out on both ends. Teaching our children that they are spiritual entities connected to God, and yet live in physical bodies that require care, will help them learn to live a life of balance and good choices.

The health of the body is so important that, even after Jesus' ascension, the apostles are able to carry on His work of healing. In

Acts 3:1–10 Peter heals the Crippled Beggar. We see in this passage that a healthy body, as well as the gift of healing, glorifies God. Illness can often impede our ability to do God's work. Helping our children maintain good health throughout their lives allows them the freedom to live for God. Teaching them to treat their bodies,

> The God who made the world and everything in it is the Lord of heaven and earth and does not live in temples built by hands.
>
> Acts 17:24

and one another's bodies, as temples to the Holy Spirit translates into a mind, body, soul, and spirit ready to be devoted to our Lord.

A Lying Tongue

There is an adage that says, "If you can't say anything nice, don't say anything at all." This easily captures one of those qualities that provide a satisfying, peaceful

> *Therefore guard against profitless grumbling, and from lie with your tongues; For a stealthy utterance does not go unpunished, and a lying mouth slays the soul.*
>
> *Book of Wisdom 1:11*

> *By your words you will be acquitted, and by your words you will be condemned.*
>
> *Matthew 12:37*

> *Keep your tongue from evil, your lips from speaking lies. Turn from evil and do good; seek peace and pursue it.*
>
> *Psalm 34:14–15*

> *The lying tongue is its owner's enemy, and the flattering mouth works ruin.*
>
> *Proverbs 26:28*

adulthood. Found over and over again in scripture is the message that our tongues need to be guarded lest they be the cause of great trouble in our lives. Haven't we experienced this ourselves? Don't we all know the trouble our words can get us into? As we have seen in other areas, words are incredibly powerful tools with the ability to build up or to tear down. It is, quite simply, up to us which way our children learn to use their words. But first they must see themselves as they really are. They must realize how they use their words and the effect their words have on their peers, the adults in their lives, and the people they encounter.

Children today have many ways in which to learn the value of their words. As adults who understand the intrinsic power of words, we need to use every opportunity to relay this understanding to our children. Helping them choose kind, compassionate, and honest words has many benefits. Teaching how powerful words are begins to create an understanding of a "reap what you sow" existence. When children are encouraged to take conse-

> *Discuss your case with your neighbor, but another man's secret do not disclose.*
> *Proverbs 25:9*
>
> *The false witness will not go unpunished and he who utters lies will not escape.*
> *Proverbs 19:5*
>
> *You shall not bear false witness against your neighbor.*
> *Exodus 20:16*

quences for their actions, they are also encouraged to avoid slanderous, blaming words. When we encourage them to avoid using judgmental words we are actually helping them avoid judgment as well. When we teach our children to use words of praise to the Lord for their earthly achievements, we are truly teaching them to avoid a life filled with God-less pride.

Fire and Brimstone

When we read scripture it is easy to imagine fire and brimstone preachers who both intimidated and entranced people. Preachers creating images of Hell. Images that could deter immoral behavior through fear alone. Preachers who weren't politically correct or even concerned about political correctness. Preachers who were simply concerned about the salvation of souls.

Right now, as the mother of three sons, I'm not sure if that's such a bad thing! A little fear can go a long way in keeping children on track. Politically incorrect? Maybe. True? Most definitely. Unfortunately, we've been so inundated with stories of mistreatment and trauma that we've begun to dump all parental control into a bag called "abuse." We've become so concerned about our children's rights that we

> *From one man he made every nation of men, that they should inhabit the whole earth; and he determined the times set for them and the exact places where they should live. God did this so that men would seek him and perhaps reach out for him and find him, though he is not far from each one of us. For in him we live and move and have our being.*
> *Acts 17:26–27*

have forgotten their right to have parents who are "in charge." Do we need to be at the other end of the spectrum? Probably not. Is a certain amount of fear a bad thing? I don't think so. Certainly, if I have to clarify my meaning of "fear" then I am missing my intent. I would never promote harm, verbal or physical, to a child. Instead, I'm referring to helping our children recognize their strengths as well as their weaknesses. I am referring to nurturing our children in such a way that they are interested in becoming better people. People of God. People with morals, values, and integrity.

If we understand the length of eternity, don't we all want our children to spend it in Heaven? And, if we look to the bible for our guidance we will, in fact, find that the bible is neither worried about political correctness nor is it trying to sugar coat any message. Scripture tells it like it is. Fire and brimstone. Maybe that's why we currently flock to "tell-it-like-it-is" talk shows. Somewhere inside of us is the desire to live by God's rules and seek His wisdom. We're just looking in the wrong places.

Unfortunately, our children are not accustomed to this honest kind of communication. Sugar coating has become the packaging of all messages. I was recently told that, overall, our nation's children scored quite low on certain national tests and yet *felt very good* about how they did! In other words, they had no idea that they did so poorly on these tests. Having been coddled and coaxed over the past dozen years seems to have only increased our children's positive perceptions of themselves, but nothing else. And it turns out that the perception that they have of their skills is incorrect. As a parent I want my children to have positive but **honest** perceptions of themselves.

If our children do not see themselves as they really are, then they do not know their areas of weakness and need. They also do not know their **true** areas of strength and talents. If they do not know their areas of weakness and need, how will they improve? If they do not know their areas of strength and talents, how will they succeed in life?

66

Taking this a step further, what might their spiritual perceptions of themselves be? Are they able to give a true accounting of their actions? Consider the qualities that make a God-fearing person: honesty, integrity, perseverance, and generosity of spirit. If our children are not able to see themselves in a proper light, how will they come to the realization that they should be working on these spiritual qualities? Of course, this is abhorrent to many parents. The idea that children should be told of their weaknesses is attacked. However, in raising my children I just can't find one good reason to ignore their behaviors that need improvement. So, just like I compliment them on their successes, I feel obligated to guide them where they need improvement. And, like most people, they have their fair share of areas that need improvement. It is a common understanding in our household what kind of "work" each of us needs to do. I have to work on patience while one son has to work on his tone of voice and another has to work on not sulking. They also know, full well, their areas of strengths. One is amazing at the amount of time he will dedicate to mastering a skill while another is awesome at helping with chores. And so this list goes as well. I like the fact that my children know we are all "works-in progress." They also know that the joy of living is the joy found in the journey. It is setting a goal, reaching a plateau, and enjoying the sights before moving ahead. When we stop being interested in the journey we truly stop living the life Christ died to give us.

Your Child's Friendships

The ironic thing about people is that, regardless of God's hopes and plans, some are real trouble. Or they bring trouble, or they look for trouble. So, while Jesus encourages us to reach out to the "uninvitable," the downtrodden, and the lonely, the prophet Sirach reminds us to be wary of the troublemakers. These are very different people than those Jesus was talking about. Yes, God does love everyone but no, our children do not need to associate with those who will hinder them. In fact, any worthwhile parent is very aware of, and is always monitoring, his or her child's friendships. This is because friends and acquaintances can be very influential. Much more so than we would often like to admit.

I know two women whose lives have taken particular courses as a direct result of the high school friendships they forged. One had friends that "partied," while the other had friends focused on attending college. All other factors being the same (both women came from the same kind of home atmosphere and similar parental expectation) their individual friendships seemed to have a sizable impact on their life. Needless to say the woman whose friends were college oriented, did herself go to college. The other woman, whose friends had no college interests, did not attend college. I share this with you not as a judgment of the value of college but with the belief that friends do, indeed, impact bigger life issues. They are an important part of our children's lives.

> Bring not every man into your house, for many are the snares of the crafty one.
> Sirach 11:29
>
> Limit the time you spend with fools, but frequent the company of thoughtful men.
> Sirach 28:12
>
> Beware of false prophets, who come to you in sheep's clothing, but underneath are ravenous wolves.
> Matthew 7:15

With this in mind, I believe it is important to be very aware of your child's relationships. Encouraging your child to invite the "uninvitable" does not mean allowing him or her to indulge in unwise friendships. Remember that downtrodden is a very different adjective than crafty or underhanded. I think that many acquaintances can actually open your child to influences that have great potential for harm. This is a subtle way of saying that the devil is always looking for a way in and there is no reason to open the door. Compound peer pressure and temptation with a poor choice in friends and you have a sure-fire recipe for disaster.

As parents, our mindfulness, combined with our prayerful intercessions, are the keys to keeping our children free from potentially harmful relationships. They need to be knowledgeable as well. A very basic part of life is to teach them how to recognize and avoid temptation and trouble, both of which come in the form of people, places, and things. Our children need to learn how to stay on the right (Matthew 7:13–14). "Enter through the narrow gate. For wide is the gate and broad is the path that leads to destruction, and many enter through it. But small is the gate and narrow the road that leads to life, and only a few find it." Our children should also be aware that their decisions, good and bad, will most definitely have consequences. Essentially we want them to know that life is full of opportunities that lead to sin and equip them with the tools to choose otherwise.

Of course prayer is a strong defense to help keep our children on course. One of my petitions to the Lord goes something like this, "Father, thank you for all the friends in my children's lives. May they always be pleasing to you and have your anointing. May all my children's friendships bring them closer to you." This is coupled with the honest discussions we have about ways to conduct ourselves. Friendships are a two way street and I want my children to learn how to be the kind of friends that other people cherish. We often talk about the qualities that make a good friend and the qualities that are worth developing. My children know full well why each of my close friends are just that, close. They know the valuable characteristics that each of us is able to bring to our relationships, each with something unique. I dedicated this book to one of my dearest friends, Pam. My children know that I admire Pam as a mother and as a Christian. Although there are times when I feel I take more from the relationship than I give, Pam assures me that I bring blessings to her as well. My children know that Pam and I spend time nurturing our friendship because we recognize it as a gift from God. True Godly friendships will bring out the best in one another. This doesn't mean there won't be growing, stretching, and learning. But it will be in a way that is pleasing to God. It is valuable to remember the adage that people enter our lives for a reason, a season, or a lifetime. From this perspective we are able to help our children grow and

My brethren have withdrawn from me, and my friends are wholly estranged. My kinsfolk and companions neglect me, and my guests have forgotten me.
Job 19:13-14

He said to his disciples, "things that cause sin will inevitably occur, but woe to the person through whom they occur."
Luke 17:1

He who touches pitch blackens his hand; he who associates with an impious man learns his ways.
Sirach 13:1

mature as Christians with the help of the people God brings into their lives.

Finally, my children are well aware of why they are not allowed certain friendships or why other friendships are on a limited basis. Additionally, they know why certain friendships have my blessing. From my perspective, this is teaching my children to make wise choices as far as their own actions are concerned. While this is not always an easy task, I do my best to help my children make wise friendship choices. Of course, I remain as vigilant as possible and continue praying. Sometimes, maybe even more often than I would like, I feel like the "bad guy" because of my restrictions. However, I also have to be accountable for my decisions as a parent and

> *A good tree does not bear rotten fruit, nor does a rotten tree bear good fruit. For every tree is know by its own fruit. For people do not pick figs from thornbushes, nor do they gather grapes from brambles. A good person out of the store of goodness in his heart produces good, but an evil person out of a store of evil produces evil; for from the fullness of the heart the mouth speaks.*
> *Luke 6:43–45*

that realization outweighs my hopes that my children will understand and accept all my decisions. I make my decision based upon the belief that children should be at the giving and receiving end of worthwhile relationships. They learn this skill and its value from us. They see it in our earthly friendships and they see it in our friendship with Christ. Modeling Godly friendships will help bring anointed friendships into our children's lives.

Your Child's Character

Until about three years ago I was very driven by the grades my children received. Like most parents, my husband and I were quite focused on our children's grades. Our children's report cards drove our family agenda. Good report cards provided any extras in their lives: television, computer, Nintendo, movies etc. Bad report cards took things away. The difficulty was that a good report card was an all "A" report card with maybe one "B." Everything else was a bad report card. Looking back it seems hard to believe that I could force these standards on my kids. Nonetheless, I share this with you to make a point of the depth of my new perspective on grades.

Grades are still important to me. I expect my children to go to college. I would like to see each one attend a recognized, big name college. I would like to see my boys all become successful professionals. I want the best for my children. But more important, I want all the great things that God has in store for them. And that's the key right now. I want all that God has in store for them. There is no doubt in my heart that God has great things in store for my children. However, I finally realize that God's great plans may very well be different than mine. Additionally, I understand that while grades are important, they are only a piece of the life my children are forging. There are so many things that are more important to my children's future.

I have come to value their non-academic traits as much as, if not more than, their academic abilities. I have begun to see that the characteristics that are of real value include kindness, compassion, honesty, integrity, enthusiasm, endurance, wisdom, and patience. The more I read scripture the more I see the tremendous emphasis that is placed on these and other "non-academic" traits. I have learned to temper my academic expectations with non-academic aspirations. I have learned to embrace more of the difficult opportunities that my children encounter; situations in which I know they can grow and learn. It is a fine line between protection and sheltering but it is a line that parents should cross less often. We want to protect our children against true harm and societal woes but not at the expense of thriving. Consider our children as delicate plants that are faced with an unexpected spring frost. While we cover them to provide them with protection, we don't uproot them until the frost passes. Life is filled with many unexpected frosts. With compassionate authority we will cover our children to protect them but should not uproot them until the frost passes.

Pay to all their dues, taxes to whom taxes are due, toll to whom toll is due, respect to whom respect is due, honor to whom honor is due.

Romans 13:7

Let not kindness and fidelity leave you; bind them around your neck; Then will you win favor and good esteem before God and man.

Proverbs 3:4

Do not neglect hospitality, for through it some have unknowingly entertained angels. Be mindful of prisoners as if sharing their imprisonment, and of the ill-treated as of yourselves, for you also are in the body . . . Let your life be free from love of money but be content with what you have, for he has said, "I will never forsake you or abandon you."

Hebrews 13:1–3,5

Scripture recounts the stories of many people who had to endure difficult trials before they could be of use to God. Trials in which they remained faithful to God even though He seemed to have abandoned them. When most people think of trial and tribulation, they think of the story of Job. And rightly so. Job's story encourages us to remain faithful to God in all of our life's circumstances. However, I find the story of Joseph to be quite compelling as well. Here's a young man who is hated by his brothers because of his father's favoritism. Their hatred is so deep that they plot to kill him (Genesis 37:18) but eventually sell him into slavery for twenty shekels of silver (Genesis 37:28). The parallel here to Jesus is remarkable. God, as He always does, brings good out of even the worst circumstances and we see that Joseph prospers (Genesis 39:2). In another turn of events, typical in life, Joseph ends up in prison (Genesis 39:20). From there, God once again works the details and Joseph eventually ends up in a situation where he will be able to save his brothers (the original bad guys) from a famine that is sweeping the nation (Genesis 41:40).

We see how trials allowed people to deepen their relationship with God. They allow us and our children to grow into disciples of Christ. No matter how we look at it, trials and tribulations allow us to advance in unimaginable ways.

School is a great proving ground for handling complex circumstances. Time and again our children are confronted by situations where they must rely on the characteristics shown to us by Joseph and Job. School provides countless opportunities for our children to develop their moral muscles. Along with a day-to-day school life that includes bullying, teacher's pets,

> *So then each of us shall give an account of himself to God.*
>
> *Romans 14:12*
>
> *You have been weighed on the scales and found wanting.*
>
> *Daniel 5:27*
>
> *A good name is more desirable than great riches, and high esteem, than gold and silver.*
>
> *Proverbs 22:1*

and a variety of cliques, school seems to be a time when our children are thrown into group dynamics that are difficult at best. I often listen to these stories and remind myself of the stories of Job and Joseph. My belief is that, if I am able to guide my children through these challenging situations, God will help them prosper from the experiences. I remind myself that these encounters often hold a greater value than is immediately apparent. That is why the classroom is often an opportune playing field. It provides great practice for life and countless ways in which our children will be challenged to develop their Christ-like characteristics of patience, charity, forgiveness, and perseverance. As long as there isn't a situation that is truly harmful, I know my children will learn from these trying times. After all, life is really about learning to live and work with others. Life is about moving forward when the forces seem to be holding us back. Jesus tells us that there is a great and bountiful harvest but there aren't enough workers. It is our job to help our children become the workers Jesus is looking for. He says, *"The harvest is plentiful but the workers are few." Matthew 9:37.* Let our children learn to work in such a way as they may enjoy the harvest.

Of course we seem to live in a world where Christ-like characteristics are neither embraced nor nurtured. It is becoming increasingly difficult, even impossible, to raise an innocent child. And yet, it is a goal about which we

> *Be merciful, just as your Father is merciful.*
> *Luke 6:36*

must be diligent. Whenever possible we should realize that our words and actions need to reflect the qualities that we want to develop in our children. While standing our moral ground we should be showing patience and kindness to a loving neighbor as well as an irritating driver or rude store clerk. We would do well to model compassion and generosity at every turn. When we understand the Word of God we are able to cultivate our moral ground in a way that allows us firm footing. As I mentioned earlier, parenting shouldn't be shifting and swaying. If we are led by an understanding of the Word of God, we recognize the stability in the fruit that our life should bear. God's Word simply does not change. What was right yesterday continues to be right today and will most certainly be right tomorrow.

Along with a firm moral foundation, children should also be encouraged to live with gratitude. When we consider the traits that we are developing in our children, we would do well to acknowledge that gratitude creates a person who can be happy within a moment instead of always assuming happiness is just around the corner. This is a wonderful and valuable trait for a child to develop. Indeed, it is a wonderful and valuable trait for us all to develop.

As we raise our children we want to continually acknowledge the necessity of developing their "non-academic" qualities. We should be trying to raise our children as true Christians, as true followers of Christ. They will find success in their earthly lives if they understand their worth in Christ and their obligation to their fellow man. Consequently, a combination of academic and non-academic traits really are necessary to cultivate in our children. We want them to understand that they are "on this earth but not of this earth," as scripture tells us. We are teaching them skills to live fruitful, successful, and moral lives.

Reap What You Sow

Nothing seems more easily conveyed than this message: *Reap What You Sow*. Every action has an equal and opposite reaction. Karma. As you have done, so shall it be done to you. Do to others whatever you would have them do to you. Blessed are the merciful for they will be shown mercy. What goes around, comes around. A tit for a tat. We have all heard the jargon. No matter how we look at it, this happens to be a scripture message that exists on many different levels and in many different environments.

For us, as Christian parents, this is a mighty message for our children. In many ways it helps us teach our children the impact of free will and how to use it. Our free will makes us co-creators of our earthly existence. How powerful is that? And our earthly decisions and existence determine our eternity. In other words, we really will cause our own judgment. So, what we choose to do in any given situation is, as trite as it sounds, up to us. And the impact is far-reaching. Furthermore, if our children see there is a real connection between their actions and the consequences, they are much more likely to make better decisions. Scripture tells us that things will be done to us as we have done to others. Simple, yet powerful.

So, how do we incorporate this into the lives of our children? First and foremost I believe that children should fully understand and live by the golden rule. It really is that uncomplicated. And, if we add to that our own actions to reinforce our words, we have created a powerful message based squarely on scripture.

To that end, it is important to share with your child your thoughts, actions, and reactions. This allows your child to see connections he or she might otherwise miss. One technique I use in the classroom is to share my thinking "out loud." This helps the students see how I am looking at information, gathering data, discarding extraneous facts and then putting things together. I have also noticed a direct link between "aha" moments and class discussions. Students become animated when they make connections based on observations and interpretations that they share. They feed off each other and the payoff is tremendous. We need to do the same thing for our children. Letting our children "hear" us thinking helps them develop their thinking process. Letting our children "hear" us weighing the consequences is quite telling. Letting our children see that we believe that our actions will cause reactions is powerful.

Recently a few friends took a trip. Although invited, we were unable to join them. Between work schedules and various commitments, the timing was just not right. I found myself torn between bouts of jealousy and my desire to wish them a safe, fun, and wonderful trip. With God's grace I was able to move into a peaceful place where I was able to wholeheartedly pray for them

> *Do to others whatever you would have them do to you.*
> *Matthew 8:12*
>
> *Consider this: whoever sows sparingly will also reap sparingly, and whoever sows bountifully will also reap bountifully.*
> *2 Corinthians 9:6*
>
> *Do to others as you would have them do to you.*
> *Luke 6:31*

and their trip. I asked God to give them all the aspects of a vacation that make it memorable and cherished. In praying I was able to forget about my own desires. My whole heart wanted them to have an awesome vacation. I stood up from that prayer feeling a deep sense of peace and contentment.

Then, of course, the most miraculous thing happened. I say "of course" because God never ceases to let us down. That afternoon my father called. He lives in Oregon. He called to offer to make arrangements for my two youngest sons and myself to spend a week in Oregon! So, quite literally, my husband could not take time off work and my oldest son was starting a new job and shouldn't be taking a vacation and here I was being offered a vacation for the three people in my family who could take a vacation! Reap what you sow. From deep in my heart I sowed the seeds for others to have a beautiful vacation and I reaped the harvest immediately! Sometimes it really is that simple. Of course we have since taken the trip and we had a wonderful time. We have the cherished memories that I prayed for my friends to have. We relaxed and spent time sightseeing. God heard the words of my heart and allowed us to harvest them. We spent time with my father, enjoyed the beauty of Oregon, and recognized the hand of God throughout the entire week. It was exactly what I had prayed for, except it was a prayer I had said for other people.

In this particular example the direct connection between my heart's desire for our friends to have a beautiful trip and my dad's

> *Make no mistake: God is not mocked for a person will reap only what he sows, because the one who sows for his flesh will reap corruption from the flesh but the one who sows for the spirit will reap eternal life from the spirit.*
> Galatians 6:7–8

> *As a stone falls back on him who throws it up, so a blow struck in treachery injures more than one. As he who digs a pit falls into it, and he who lays a snare is caught in it, whoever does harm will be involved in it, without knowing how it came upon him.*
> Sirach 28:25–27

offer of a trip brought me to tears. Learning to see the connections is a part of the learning process. These are the connections that we want to recognize and share with our children. Coincidence is no longer a part of my vocabulary. I believe that to say things are a "coincidence" is an insult to God's working in my life. My friend sent me a cute email that read something like this: "Coincidence is what it is called when God wishes to remain anonymous."

> *Blessed are the merciful, for they will be shown mercy.*
> *Matthew 5:7*
>
> *Let us not grow tired of doing good, for in due time we shall reap our harvest, if we do not give up.*
> *Galatians 6:9*
>
> *As you have done, so shall it be done to you.*
> *Obidiah 15*

Ultimately I believe that our heart is how God hears us, views us, seeks us, and speaks to us. Encourage your child to sow from his or her heart and God will be an active participant in your child's life. "Blessed are the clean of heart for they will see God." Matthew 5:8

Wisdom

Wisdom and understanding are truly incredible, seemingly rare human characteristics. Scripture says to acquire these qualities at the sake of gold and silver (Proverbs 16:16). King Solomon was said to have been extremely wise. Consider how he settled the issue over the baby (1 Kings 3:16–28). He is confronted with two women who are claiming motherhood of a newborn baby. Apparently both women delivered babies at the same time but one of the babies died shortly thereafter. Now both women are claiming that the one surviving baby is hers. To settle this difficult dispute King Solomon issues the following order, "Cut the living child in two, and give half to one woman and half to the other." How intriguing. But of course, in King Solomon's *wisdom* he has great *understanding* of a mother's selfless love and, just as he expected, the birth mother says, "Please, my lord, give her the living child-please do not kill it!" Meanwhile, the imposter agrees to this decision. At this point King Solomon knows who the real mother is and the baby is returned to her. Very wise.

We know that using wisdom helps reduce or eliminate all kinds of potential or existing problems in life. As parents we try to be as wise as Solomon when solving disputes in our house, at work, or between our children. Although I'm sure we don't succeed quite as much as he did we appreciate the value of wisdom nonetheless.

We try to use our own wisdom to help our children in all aspects of their life. Knowing the value of wisdom and understanding we should make a conscious effort to help our children acquire these traits. Like all lessons from scripture, wisdom is very much tied to other characteristics that we want to develop in our children. For instance, scripture helps us understand that a wise person holds his tongue. That

How much better to acquire wisdom than gold! To acquire understanding is more desirable than silver.
Proverbs 16:16

When all Israel heard the judgment the king had given, they were in awe of him, because they saw that the king had in him the wisdom of God for giving judgment.
1 Kings 3:28

The mind of the wise man makes him eloquent, and augments the persuasiveness of his lips.
Proverbs 16:23

But wisdom delivered from tribulation those who served her.
Wisdom 10:9

is because a wise person is aware of the power of spoken words. Don't we all have experiences where we have seen the true impact of our words? It might have been in a consoling, loving way or it might have been in an angry, hostile way. But we have certainly had the experience where our words have made a difference in someone's life. When you are wise you are careful as to the words you use and how you use them. Also remember that diligence and perseverance are wise ways to conduct oneself. Wisdom should be our guiding force.

Wisdom comes from experience and from learning history. Wisdom comes with age (sometimes). According to scripture, wisdom is to be sought at all costs. I love this proverb: *A smart man learns from his mistakes but a wise man learns from others' mis-*

takes. This captures what we want for our children. Again, this is where the value of scripture is priceless.

Scripture has commentary on every human quality, characteristic, and trait imaginable. A wise parent turns to scripture to gain an understanding of God's laws, expectations, and wishes. In doing so a parent helps ensure that his or her children will be wise and pleasing to God. Additionally, God will manifest many opportunities from which our children may gain wisdom. In fact, because He loves them and is so wonderful He will continue to present them with the same dilemma, over and over, until they get it right. Until they *wise* up! I certainly see this at work in my own life. For our children, wisdom comes from the experiences they have at school, at work, and at home. We should then, as parents, diligently help them pursue and gain wisdom.

> *And I saw that wisdom has the advantage over folly as much as light has the advantage over darkness.*
> Ecclesiastes 2:13

> *Weep but a little over the dead man, for he is at rest, but worse than death is the life of a fool.*
> Sirach 22:10

> *Get wisdom, get understanding! Do not forget or turn aside from the words I utter. Forsake her not, and she will preserve you; love her, and she will safeguard you, The beginning of wisdom is: get wisdom; at the cost of all you have, get understanding.*
> Proverbs 4:5–7

Diligence and Perseverance

School provides a wonderful arena to sow the seeds of diligence and perseverance. School provides countless opportunities for you to teach your child the value of hard work, dedication, and overcoming obstacles. Whether it be from a teacher that your child does not get along with or a game that your child cannot master, perseverance is the name of the school game!

May the God of endurance and encouragement grant you to think in harmony with one another, in keeping with Christ Jesus...

Romans 15:5

He who tills his own land has food in plenty, but he who follows idle pursuits is a fool.

Proverbs 12:11

Not only that, but we even boast of our afflictions, knowing that affliction produces endurance, and endurance, proven character, and proven character, hope, and hope does not disappoint...

Romans 5:3–5

This is a time to teach your child to draw from inner God-given strengths and take great wisdom from life's teaching moments.

If you purposely set about determining the values you want to instill in your child you will be amazed at how many ways will arrive for you to teach that lesson! Of course we all look at our opportunities in assorted ways. Parents are no different. Parents respond diversely to the same set of circumstances. I believe that these differences arrive from the distinct lessons or values that the parents hold in esteem. For instance, there are always students who simply do not do the assigned work for my class. Regardless of the assignment, excuse, or student, this is just a given in a middle school classroom. What changes however, is the way that the different parents will deal with the same situation.

Most impressive (and I believe most wise) are the parents who will still require that their children do late assignments. These parents are not focused on the grade or teaching their child to walk away because a grade is no longer attainable. These parents are giving their children a powerful message. They are saying that a strong work ethic, that doing the right thing, outweighs a grade. These parents understand that this experience is providing an opportunity to instill a sense of commitment and dedication in their children. These children are learning that they must persevere and see things through to the end. These children are being taught the value of diligence and a strong work ethic.

Then there is another camp of parents who deal differently with this situation. These parents will fight with a teacher for one reason or another or simply allow their kids to abandon the work altogether. This also gives a strong message. Children of these parents are learning to circumvent the system. These parents are teaching their children to go around, under, and over but not straight through. They are not making use of an opportunity to build a strong work ethic in their child.

The same opportunity, handled differently, produces different results. Scripture tells us the value of diligence and perseverance. Diligence and perseverance are characteristics that will carry a child through his or her whole life. Consider Job's great rewards after he got through all of the hardships that came his way. He persevered and God delivered him. Not only did God deliver Job but God blessed him beyond imagination. Learning how to see things through to the end and getting through difficult circumstances builds great character. Children have enough influences to be wily, sly, and underhanded. Parents should never present an opportunity for their children to be less than moral and forthright. Diligence and perseverance are not for the faint of heart and that is why they are truly valuable characteristics to develop in our children.

My son took Japanese in his freshman year of high school. Japanese is an extremely difficult language to learn. The dropout and failing rate of this language class is easily triple that of other language classes. Unlike many other languages, Japanese requires that the student must learn the characters of the language as well as the pronunciation and grammar. Anyhow, mid-year the students were all given an opportunity to withdraw. Believe me, my son wanted to be at the head of the exodus. This posed a real dilemma for us because this Japanese class was going to clearly bring down his high grade point average. On the other hand, both my husband and I agreed that letting him withdraw simply gave the wrong message at this impressionable age. So, after much discussion, we *firmly* recommended that he do his best and stay with the class. Although his heart was really not in the second semester of Japanese, we felt it was the right thing to have him do. We were faced

> *Let us not grow tired of doing good, for in due time we shall reap our harvest, if we do not give up.*
> *Galatians 6:9*
>
> *Only everyone should live as the Lord has assigned, just as God called each one.*
> *1 Corinthians 7:17*

89

with an "easy out" or what we considered the "right thing to do." We opted for the "right thing to do" and have not looked back. Yes, his grade point average was impacted, but so was his understanding of diligence and perseverance.

When my middle son was in fifth grade he was assigned an interesting social studies project. He had to research a particular event and then create a travel brochure for it. I thought the assignment was imaginative and enjoyed helping him gather information. I was pleased with the amount of time he put into it and thought the end product was quite excellent. He learned quite a bit from the assignment. Needless to say he received a "B" on the brochure. Although he was a bit deflated by the grade I felt it was a great opportunity to help him recognize that he really did put his best work into the brochure and that he could be proud of what he did. Plain and simple. Additionally, it was important that he had no animosity toward the teacher for this grade. His role as student was to do his best and ask questions to help him accomplish this. I encouraged him to ask his peers to see which brochures earned "A's" so that he could learn for next time. Teaching children to "look around" and learn is a tactic I use with my own children and encourage in my students as well. Do your very best and learn from others along the way. I try to remember that the smart man learns from his own mistakes but the wise man learns from others'! In this instance, I did not want my son to put blame on the teacher or discount himself or his work. He had worked diligently and could be proud of that fact. On the other hand the teacher felt there were ways in which he could improve and that was valuable too. I believe it is unfair to allow children to always think they have produced the perfect paper, an excellent report, or a superior project. This is not helping them become better thinkers or doers. In our effort to shelter our children from disagreeable circumstances or fair and honest criticism, we have really done a disservice

> *The soul of the sluggard craves in vain, but the diligent soul is amply satisfied.*
>
> *Proverbs 13:4*

to them. The pendulum has swung too far in the opposite direction. So, my son knew how proud I was of his work but that there was still an opportunity for him to learn.

I think it is especially important to remember that school is a springboard for life. Consider all you know about relationships and careers. Now look at school as an incredible opportunity to teach about these things. Look at what skills you know your children will

> *The slothful become impoverished, but the diligent gain wealth.*
> Proverbs 12:16

need to enter the job force and enjoy a successful career. What do they need to enjoy rewarding relationships with friends, family and eventually a spouse? Consider school the best battle field for work, relationships, and life. School is filled with occasions to show compassion, wisdom, dedication, commitment, empathy, kindness, and integrity. We will be given countless opportunities to instill these characteristics in our children as they move through their school years. When we make the most of these years we help our children build a strong foundation in which to move into the world.

Fruits of the Spirit

One of the first assignments I had for my Master's degree was to write a mission statement for my class room. After getting past the notion that this was a silly assignment for a veteran teacher, I surprisingly found myself in a quandary. I knew in my heart what I wanted my mission statement to be but was perplexed when I read it on paper. It seemed so trite, almost ludicrous.

Essentially, I felt that a classroom that was filled with kindness, joy, and compassion would help all students achieve success. Based on my experience as a teacher of both adolescents and adults I knew first hand how detrimental a lack of kindness was for any student, regardless of age. The way I saw it, compassion and kindness mixed with joy created an environment where each student could feel brave enough to take risks: whether that meant asking questions, reading out loud, or writing on the board. Once a student could feel free to take risks, success was sure to follow. I have found that a student (child or adult) too fearful to take a step forward, will obviously go nowhere. So, my mission statement, as trite as it sounded, remained intact.

Now, more than ever, I see that same mission statement as steeped in scripture and of the utmost importance. Students actually do perform better when they are able to feel enough confidence to step outside of their weaknesses and take a risk. Again, this might be something as simple as raising a hand to ask a question and not be worried that peers will roll their eyes. Or, it might be as bold as taking a leadership role for a normally shy and quiet student. What could be better than knowing your child is helping create a kind, compassionate environment from which his or her peers may excel? That is truly awesome.

Rejoice with those who rejoice, weep with those who weep.
Romans 12:15

Every tree that does not bear good fruit will be cut down and thrown into the fire.
Matthew 4:10

For each man's ways are plain to the Lord's sight; all their paths he surveys; By his own iniquities the wicked man will be caught, in the meshes of his own sin he will be held fast; He will die from lack of discipline, through the greatness of his folly he will be lost.
Proverbs 5:21–23

Unfortunately, this is the exact opposite message that our children are fed in their television programs, games they play, music they listen to, sports they play, and friendships they forge. In fact, these things often promote selfishness, greed, and avarice. People are rewarded for rudeness, egocentrism, and cunning. Raising a child based upon scripture virtues can be a very difficult task indeed. However, your diligence as a parent may be the only hope your child has of learning Christ's way. This is, quite frankly, a huge responsibility. Knowing and teaching the fruits of the Spirit (love, joy, peace, patience, kindness, generosity, faithfulness, gentleness, self-control) is the best defense against an ominous secularism.

Not only are we told to develop and produce the fruits of the spirit but we have also been told that we will reap what we sow.

Frankly, that gives us all the more reason to encourage our children to practice the Christian attributes of love, joy, peace, patience, kindness, generosity, faithfulness, gentleness, and self-control. To help our children learn this we must remember that our actions are as important as our words. Our children need to witness us as joyful and self-controlled adults. They need to witness us displaying the fruits of the spirit in our everyday actions. Do we let people into our lane with a smile and a blessing? Do we allow someone to get ahead of us in check out if they only have a few items and we have a basketful? Do our children hear us share stories of others with compassion for their situation, or do we sound judgmental? Do our children see us pick up the neighbor's fallen garbage cans? How joyful and faithful are we in any given day? How are we showing our children the fruits of our spirit? When we make a conscious effort to bring these attributes more fully into our lives, all those around us benefit. We, then, make the best examples for our children to follow.

Matthew 5:16 reminds us that people should see our good deeds so that the Father can be glorified. This is very different from any message our children receive. Our children tend towards their own glory, which we as a society have tremendously encouraged. What we want is for our children to develop a healthy sense of worth in Christ and an understanding that all glory and honor truly do belong to God. Whatever gifts He has given our children are theirs for the

> *Blessed are the peacemakers, for they will be called children of God.*
> *Matthew 5:9*
>
> *Just so, your light must shine before others, that they may see your good deeds and glorify your heavenly Father.*
> *Matthew 5:16*

taking but must ultimately be for His glory. Our children should learn to offer all things up to Christ, for His glory, and with gratitude.

Often times we are moved by the Holy Spirit towards an act of kindness but "think better of it" and then pass on the God-given opportunity. Move with the Spirit when the Spirit is moving you. I always enjoy shopping during after season clearance times. This past Christmas I found a beautiful embroidered angel pillow for 75% off the original price. It was very pretty and since I love angel-anything, I bought it. When I paid for the pillow the gal at the check out commented on it and asked if there were any more. She seemed to genuinely like the pillow. I agreed how pretty it was and told her I had the perfect place for it. I paid and walked away. About 30 feet from the register I turned around, looked her way, and then turned around again. I'm sure any onlookers thought I was a bit confused as I turned around a second time and then turned around again. Finally, I turned a third time and headed back toward the register. My mind was made up and the pillow was in hand. I actually apologized to the lady (I didn't want her to think I was crazy) and told her I just felt that the pillow should be hers. I felt completely led by the Spirit to give her the pillow. Although I was very intent on talking myself out of that gesture I am forever grateful that I didn't. It was awesome to be led by the Spirit. And, I believe that when we follow the Spirit we are given more opportunities to do just that. When we shut down that line of communication, we begin to lose those God-given moments to connect with other people in a very spiritual way. But it is important to remember that there is no magic formula for the Spirit to be a part of your life or your child's life. As a friend recently said to me, "let go and let God." So, I say to you, *Let go and Let God and in all ways, let the Holy Spirit guide you and your child.*

> *In contrast, the fruit of the Spirit is love, joy, peace, patience, kindness, generosity, faithfulness, gentleness, self-control.*
> *Galatians 5:22*
>
> *But to you who hear I say, love your enemies, do good to those who hate you, bless those who curse you, pray for those who mistreat you. To the person who strikes you on one cheek, offer the other one as well, and from the person who take your cloak, do not withhold even your tunic. Give to everyone who asks of you, and from the one who take what is yours do not demand it back.*
> *Luke 6:27–30*

Judgment

Scripture is very clear on the subject of judgment. Our own judgment will be based upon our judgment of others. From a young age we want our children to know that judgment of others is wrong. They are not in a position to judge. Nor are we. *For judgment comes not from the east or west, not from the desert or from the mountains, but from God who decides, who brings some low and raises others high. Psalm 75:7–8*

Stop judging, that you may not be judged. For as you judge, so will you be judged, and the measure with which you measure will be measured out to you. Why do you notice the splinter in your brother's eye, but do not perceive the wooden beam in your own eye?

Matthew 7:1–3

Why then do you judge your brother? Or you, why do you look down on your brother? For we shall all stand before the judgment seat of God...So then each of us shall give an account of himself to God.

Romans 14:10,12

Our job is to teach our children the difference between making a wise judgment call and having a judgmental attitude towards people or situations. They are very different. One is based on looking at facts or information and making a sound, intelligent choice while the other is putting on an air of authority that belongs solely to God. For instance, we want our children to make good choices in friends. To do this they will find themselves in a situation where they have to "judge" another's behavior. This, though, is very different than an attitude of judgment toward or about that person. This is a fine line that can often confuse adults and yet we must teach it to our children.

As with all things, a change in our words and actions will greatly influence our children. When we begin to fully incorporate scripture into our lives, and the lives of our family, we will see that the characteristics that separate us from God will begin to fall away. In particular we will be less inclined to judge others. When we make a concerted effort to stay on God's path, not veering left and not veering right (Deuteronomy 5:32), we will be showered with graces and blessings that will make our journey a successful one. Our time will be occupied with living for the glory of God and out of love for Him we will not judge others. I have a dear friend who has been quite influential in showing me the difference between doing something out of obligation and doing something out of love. When we operate out of love for

Nor does the Father judge anyone, but he has given all judgment to his Son, so that all may honor the Son just as they honor the Father. Whoever does not honor the Son does not honor the Father who sent him.

John 5:22–23

I tell you, on the day of judgment people will render an account for every careless word they speak. By your words you will be acquitted, and by your words you will be condemned.

Matthew 12:36–37

Jesus, our harmful behaviors that are a hindrance to that relationship start melting away. We would see others as Jesus does and would not be inclined to judge them. We would see them with loving eyes.

This is why our children should have a deep, established relationship with Jesus. Loving Jesus and living for Jesus, our ultimate judge (John 5:22), will help keep our inclinations to judge others under control. The deeper and more established our relationship with Jesus is, the more we see Him as existing in every human we encounter. This is a great way for our children to interact with others; understanding that each is an embodiment of Christ.

Your Treasure

This past year I received the best Mother's Day gift ever. At the time my sons were 10, 12 and 15 years old. They made a Mother's Day card (always the best kind) and each boy signed the card with a promise to do the rosary with me. There are a couple of reasons that this gift was so special.

First, I was delighted that my boys would give of themselves so selflessly for something that they find less than thrilling. Let me be honest, my boys do not like it when I say, "Let's do the rosary." They moan and groan as if I had said, "Let's replace all the shingles on the roof." So, this gift struck me as very selfless. Second, I was delighted because I realized that they had to have been on speaking terms for at least a few minutes to come up with the present and card! So, for these two reasons, I consider that Mother's Day gift the best present ever.

Of course, the real miracle was that my children knew what I treasured! I felt like my job, in many ways, was complete. That sounds a bit odd and yet that gift showed me that my children know what I love. They know I love my faith. And at their ages I believe that is the best gift I can give them. They know that my faith is my life. They see it in the books I read, the shows I watch, the friends I have, and the way I spend my time. They know how my faith helps me in my journey to become a better mother and person. What it boils down to is the idea that my children know where my treasure is and I am convinced that helps them build their own treasures as well.

Children today need to know what is truly valuable, what is truly worth their time and energy. Without a doubt my kids have very regular "kid" lives: they play sports, go to movies, play computer games, and long for fast, expensive cars. However, my husband and I do our best to help our

> *Do not store up for yourselves treasures on earth, where moth and decay destroy, and thieves break in and steal. But store up treasures in heaven, where neither moth nor decay destroys, nor thieves break in and steal. For where your treasure is, there also your heart be.*
> Matthew 6:19-21

> *Jesus said to him, "If you wish to be perfect go, sell what you have and give to the poor, and you will have treasure in heaven.*
> Matthew 19:21

> *Thus it will be for the one who stores up treasure for himself but is not rich in what matters to God.*
> Luke 12:21

> *For where your treasure is, there also will your heart be.*
> Luke 12:34

children keep these pleasures and interests in perspective. I have come to realize that part of keeping things in perspective is denial. In fact, denial is a great way for children to learn to discipline their desires, to learn self-control (a fruit of the Spirit). Denial not because you can't afford something or don't have the time but denial because you can afford something and are teaching a valuable lesson. Denial because you do have the time and ability but your children need to learn that they don't get everything all the time. If we allow our children to fill their lives with things other than God, how will we teach them to make room for God? God's graces can only abound in your child's life when your child's life abounds in God.

I feel very confident that I have achieved a fair balance between placating my children's desires and helping them become disciplined young men. Of course they might not see the balance but I'm not worried about that right now! My heart tells me what is right for my children and I thank the Holy Spirit for the help He is giving me. I try to instill in my children the fact that scripture very clearly tells us that our treasure is with God. In the meantime they still have skateboards, computers, and go to the movies but along the way there are no mixed messages. Our treasure is with God.

Consider all the messages in opposition to this. We don't see many advertisements that encourage us to build a relationship with God. In general our faith isn't affirmed through television, music, or entertainment. When children are inundated with messages contrary to finding their treasure with God, they begin to live a life filled with empty pursuits. Children can very easily be set upon a path of trying to fill a natural longing for God with material rewards and possessions. Our culture is exploding with self-satisfaction, gratification, and gain. And, as we all know, a longing for God cannot be filled with earthly things. That is where frustration and anxiety often come in. There is a societal belief that attaining and having things brings happiness. We may never know the physical or emotional ailments that stem from an unfulfilled need for God. How many people have tried to fill their lives with the things they are told will bring happiness and yet they are still unhappy? I believe that if we raise our children in a way that allows them to understand and pursue their treasure in God, we will be helping them build a life of peace and contentment. God simply did not intend for our lives to be filled with dread or distress. Scripture tells us that these are man-made problems, not from God.

> *The harvest is abundant but the laborers are few so ask the master of the harvest to send out laborers for his harvest.*
> *Matthew 9:37*

Too many people in our society have fallen prey to the messages of Hollywood, music videos, and advertisements. Quite happily, Satan sees our children spending their God-given time in ungodly ways. Since time is a treasure, or we could say that the present is a "present," how we allow our children to spend their time teaches them what their treasure is. So in very subtle ways our children learn to treasure those things in which they spend their time. It is to our children's benefit to monitor and guide the time they give to different pursuits and pleasures. As a generation, we have forgotten that we are the parents, we are in charge. Sadly, we have also followed a wolf in sheep's clothing. Somehow we have bought into the idea that our children are our equals. That our children should be part of the decision making process in our homes and in our schools. Once again, in an effort to right the wrongs we felt were inflicted upon us, we have gone too far in the opposite direction. We have become worried, afraid, and timid when it comes to our children. As such we are letting our children down.

> *Call to me, and I will answer you; I will tell to you things great beyond reach of your knowledge.*
> *Jeremiah 33:3*

What our children really need are strong parents, teachers, ministers, and guides. Nothing could be more timely than to stand firm in the truth found in scripture. Stand firm in the promises of scripture. The truth and promise of scripture is that there are great blessings for those who treasure God.

Humility

If we really want God to work in great and wonderful ways in our children's lives then we need to teach our children to be humble. Having said that, we should explore the true definition of humble. Humility is one of the greatest qualities a person can have. Humility is a true and deep understanding of our complete dependence on God. It is not, what we have been led to believe, being a victim or a doormat. Nothing could be further from the truth. Indeed, when we read scripture we recognize that every great man, from Moses to Jesus, was humble beyond compare. The fact is, when we lack humility God can do nothing with us. He will, however, allow us to experience situations that will help bring about our humility.

> *Now, Moses himself was by far the meekest man on the face of the earth.*
>
> *Numbers 12:3*
>
> *Therefore, that I might not become too elated, a thorn in the flesh was given to me, an angel of Satan, to beat me, to keep me from being too elated...Therefore, I am content with weaknesses, insults, hardships, persecutions, and constraints for the sake of Christ, for when I am weak, then I am strong.*
>
> *2 Corinthians 12:7,10*

He does this to allow us to participate in His life through His graces. He is our omniscient, omnipresent, and benevolent creator. We should be completely humbled by His interest in our lives and the lives of our children.

God calls each and every one of us to fulfill a purpose on earth. Part of our journey is the joyful discovery of God's will for our lives. This can be accomplished, in part, through a meek and humble temperament or spirit. God simply cannot (or might it be *will not*) work with us when we are too proud or arrogant. Sadly, our society has done a great job in convincing us that these self-serving qualities are the qualities that make a winner. And so, some people find out too late in the game that this couldn't be further from the truth. At that point they have missed many opportunities to walk with God and to enjoy the blessings that God had in store for them. When we help our children learn the real meaning of "meek and humble" we are setting them up for a life filled with God's workings, blessings, and graces. We owe our existence to God and nothing could be more humbling than that realization.

There are many ways to help our children achieve a fulfilling and successful life. This fulfillment begins with a humble and meek spirit. A spirit that God can work with. This is made very clear to us in scripture. Again and again we see the wonderful work God is able to do with people who, being meek in spirit, realize their total and complete dependence on God. And that is the real definition of humility: an understanding of complete dependence on God. This never means purposely humiliating a child or allowing a child to sink into a deeply humiliating situation to "show them." But rather, humility is a trait that simply reflects a real and loving understanding of our dependence on God.

Humility is the very opposite of pride. Pride, of course, is an inflated sense of self. A belief that we are responsible for the great and wonderful things that are part of our life. Scripture also makes sure we understand that people filled with pride lose their favor

106

with God. This is why St. Paul was so delighted to have an angel of Satan beating on him. He realized that this kept him humble and consequently useful to God. I admire St. Paul's enthusiasm and faith. As a parent our normal inclination is to protect our children from humbling experiences. However, if we could truly recognize the great value of those humbling experiences I am convinced we would embrace them. Especially once we become aware of the fact that these humbling circumstances will continue to surface until our children learn from them.

> *Man's pride causes his humiliation, but he who is humble of spirit obtains honor.*
>
> *Proverbs 29:23*
>
> *Blessed are the meek for they will inherit the land.*
>
> *Matthew 5:5*
>
> *And if my people, upon whom my name has been pronounced, humble themselves and pray, and seek my presence and turn from their evil ways, I will hear them from heaven and pardon their sins and revive their land*
>
> *2 Chronicles 7:14*

Humility, like honesty, integrity, and perseverance, is a vital component in our life with God. God knows our hearts and would like to call upon us to do His work. I once read something that really made me take notice of the value of a humble heart. Essentially it declared that God does not choose worthy men. Instead, He chooses men, based upon their hearts, and then makes them worthy. As long as we continue our full dependence on God, He will help make us worthy.

However, we learn from King Saul that, even if God has great plans for us, we can undermine those plans with pride and arrogance (1 Samuel 10-11). In fact, our free will and our lack of self-control allows us to wreak havoc in our own lives. Scripture tells us that things like misfortune and despair are not from God but from man. God wants great and wonderful things for our children and for us. We, however, will determine how things go. It is no coincidence that the word "humiliation" comes from the same base word that gives us "humble" and "humility." Certainly we can think of countless times when a lack of humbleness has led to humiliation. When we teach our children to be humble in their own eyes (and still understand their great worth in Jesus), we are nurturing a spirit that God can do great things with. One of my favorite prayers of gratitude is, "With you, God, I can do anything. Without you, God, I can do nothing." I am making sure that the Lord knows I fully depend on His existence in my life. And you can count on the fact that when I begin to lose a humble and dependent attitude I find myself in the middle of a situation that will provide a quick reminder! A reminder that allows me to be grateful and penitent at the same time.

Consider our Savior, Jesus Christ. Has there ever been anyone more humble and yet more able to claim greatness? Could He have come into the world in a more meek and unassuming way? If we can teach our children to look to this example and realize that every moment of His life was an illustration to us, we can begin to understand the need for our children to take on a more humble and meek demeanor. Or we can look to St. Paul who, having once been proud and arrogant, understands the need for humility in his life. St. Paul understands that he is prone to boastful and conceited ways and, because those traits will exclude God from his life, he will gladly take on humbling and humiliating circumstances. St. Paul understands these to be graces from God. For most of us, this isn't even close to how we are raising our children. We are trying to keep

> *Then I proclaimed a fast, there by the river of Ahava, that we might humble ourselves before our God to petition from him a safe journey for ourselves, our children, and all our possessions.*
> *Ezra 8:21*
>
> *Good and upright is the Lord, who shows sinners the way, Guides the humble rightly, and teaches the humble the way.*
> *Psalm 25:8-9*

them from experiencing humbling and deserving consequences, believing this is our job as parents. We are well-intentioned but ill-advised.

So, contrary to all societal messages, a humble and meek disposition is a blessing. God has great plans for the meek and kind-hearted. In fact, our children should be encouraged to help others as much as possible. Instead of coaching our children to use others as a stepping stool let us coach our children to be the stepping stool for another. Instead of sheltering our children from humbling experiences let us allow them to learn and grow in them. Instead of teaching our children to win at all costs let us teach our children a new definition of winning. We have to be brave enough, as parents, to take on this attitude. Remember that scripture tells us that those who are now first will be last and those who are last will be first. When we are first, we already have our rewards. When we encourage our children to run the race set before them with joy and confidence in the Lord, we are teaching a great lesson. We are making sure that our children live a life pursuing a noble and worthwhile treasure in God. Nothing else matters, but from that point everything else will come.

Caring for Others

God, in all His wisdom and love, continuously provides our children with opportunities to care for other people. However, our children often miss these opportunities and consequently the graces that may come from them. We need to help our children see the value, importance, and need to act upon all occasions for service.

I would give my bread to the hungry and my clothing to the naked.
Tobit 1:17

For you know the gracious act of our Lord Jesus Christ, that for your sake he became poor although he was rich, so that by his poverty you might become rich.
2 Corinthians 8:9

And the crowds asked him, "What then should we do?" He said to them in reply, "Whoever has two cloaks should share with the person who has none. And whoever has food should do likewise."
Luke 3:10-11

Matthew 25:40-46 is a passage that, by sheer brutal honesty, is both eye opening and frightening. In no uncertain terms Jesus lays down a framework for our eternity. He tells us that what we do for the "least ones" we do for Him. Who are the least ones in our children's lives? Remember that "least ones" is never a judgment call but an honest look at those in the world who need compassion and care. So, for our children that person might be a lonely classmate. It might be the student with the too curly or too short hair. Maybe it's the student who stutters. Or how about the teacher who no one likes? The neighbor who yells at everyone? The children in Africa with no clean water? Unfortunately, the list is endless. This may very well be God's way of providing us with many opportunities to do for the "least ones" and thus be pleasing before Jesus, our judge.

Trying to understand why people suffer from war, tragedy, ridicule, and starvation may truly be one of the most asked questions of our existence but not understanding why things are the way they are does not give us the right to ignore them. While we may never be able to give our children sufficient answers to those questions, we can always show our children how they can positively affect others. To turn our head from these times where we should try to make a difference is to turn our hearts as well. And that is the biggest tragedy of all.

Without a doubt, our children are surrounded by opportunities to care for others. Helping our children discover and then nurture their own God given abilities will most certainly give our children ways in which they can contribute to the care of others. For instance, a local nursing home was recently searching for middle school students who could teach the residents how to use computers, email, and other basic computer skills. What a great opportunity for kids who love computers. They are given an opportunity to pursue something they love while providing a much needed and appreciated service. Or, there is a local mental health care facility recently in need of landscape clean up and weeding. A few able-bodied teens would do wonders for themselves and the facility by embracing that opportunity. They would be able to work their muscles as well as their morals. On a bigger scale, the daughter of a very close friend recently went with her youth group to Mexico to build a house. It was a week of building and missionary work. I was impressed by her zeal and honored to be able to contribute to the funds needed for the project. This is a wonderful example of how we all bring different things to the world. While I am in no position to go build a house in Mexico, I am certainly able to lend financial support. And while the youth group had great ambition and ability to go to Mexico to build a house they had no financial means. So, when people come together, great things happen. And this is what God is counting on, even looking for. It does not matter if some pieces seem big and some pieces seem small. What does matter is that everything, every piece, is significant and necessary. So, whether it is for someone around the corner or around the world, show your children that helping others is a beautiful part of living.

> *I would give my bread to the hungry and my clothing to the naked.*
> *Tobit 1:17*

> *For you know the gracious act of our Lord Jesus Christ, that for your sake he became poor although he was rich, so that by his poverty you might become rich.*
> *2 Corinthians 8:9*

> *And the crowds asked him, "What then should we do?" He said to them in reply, "Whoever has two cloaks should share with the person who has none. And whoever has food should do likewise."*
> *Luke 3:10-11*

> *Just so, every good tree bears good fruit, and a rotten tree bears bad fruit. A good tree cannot bear bad fruit, nor can a rotten tree bear good fruit. Every tree that does not bear good fruit will be cut down and thrown into the fire. So by their fruit you will know them.*
> *Matthew 7:17–20*

Loving God

It really all begins and ends with God. The Alpha and the Omega. The beginning and the end. And so it is for us. God was with us in the beginning. He will be with us in the end. He knew us when we were formed in our mother's womb (Psalm 139:13–16). He knew our faults and sins, and still loved us into being. He made big plans and then gave us free will to choose Him and His ways. He made great blessings available in our lives. Each one of our children matters and their existence makes a difference. God doesn't see it any other way.

I feel very passionate about helping children nurture their relationship with their creator. I also believe that teaching children the awesome relationship that is available with God is a necessary part of surviving adolescence and making a success of life. God's abundant grace is available to us all. His grace allows us to share in His life in the most intimate of ways. In God, our children will truly be all that they can be. This is God's promise. With God our children will be able to live the most glorious lives filled with great blessings, graces, and eternal life. Without God our children will live lives filled with fear, anxiety, and worry. We are responsible for delivering into this world young adults who will be able to withstand temptations and dishonest ways. With God's help our children will be able to accomplish all the things necessary to make this world what it can and should be. Simply speaking, it can and should be pleasing to God.

I feel so confident in God's covenant that I implore you to rely on His Word in raising your child. Read God's edicts, understand His ways, and depend on His promises. Whenever I hear someone say, "It's all who you know." I have a sense of relief because if that's the case then we're okay. We know and glorify God! You and your children can have that same sense of relief when you help them forge a relationship with God based upon the characteristics that He cherishes: love, kindness, perseverance, humility, and wisdom to name a few. Helping our children forge a relationship with God

Hear, O Israel! The Lord is our God, the Lord alone! Therefore, you shall love the Lord, your God, with all your heart, and with all your soul, and with all your strength. Take to heart these words which I enjoin on you today. Drill them into your children. Speak of them at home and abroad, whether you are busy or at rest.
Deuteronomy 6:4–7

Love the Lord, your God, therefore, and always heed his charge: his statues, decrees and commandments.
Deuteronomy 11:1

The Lord is my shepherd; there is nothing I lack.
Psalm 23:1

is giving them a greater inheritance than gold and silver. If it is all "who you know," then who better to know than God!

Part of my teaching schedule includes teaching religion classes. I am very ardent about my faith and, to the dismay of my students, add many things to the basic curriculum. I was very surprised one day when a friend said, "I would never want to teach religion." We both share a great love of our faith and I always figured that combining my faith with my job was a real coup. So, surprise turned to dread when I heard her explanation. From her perspective my responsibility for imparting the faith to these children was something that I would be accountable for on my judgment day. After hearing her say this I was ready to quit my job. I was actually rattled to the core. What was I thinking teaching religion? Who was I to teach about Jesus? Who was I to encourage these children to love God? Who was I for any such thing? And now, here I am, trying to convince you how important scripture is in raising your children! And I still feel the same way-Who am I to write this book? Although I don't know the answer, my faith is such that if this book is God's will I know you will be reading it and will discover, or rediscover, the beauty of scripture. You will rest assured that God is with you and His grace abides in you and your children. You will know in your heart that nothing will ever separate you from the love of God in Christ Jesus our Lord (Romans 8:38-39).

My soul rests in God alone, from whom comes my salvation, God alone is my rock and salvation, my secure height; I shall never fall.
Psalm 62:2–3

Blessed is the man who trusts in the Lord, whose hope is in the Lord. He is like a tree planted beside the waters that stretches out its roots to the stream: It fears not the heat when it comes, its leaves stay green; In the year of drought it shows no distress but still bears fruit.
Jeremiah 17:7–8

Trust God and he will help you; make straight your ways and hope in him.
Sirach 2:6

Then everyone shall be rescued who calls on the name of the Lord.
Joel 3:5

To order additional copies of

Raising
Christian
Children in a
Secular World

Have your credit card ready and call:

1-877-421-READ (7323)

or please visit our web site at
www.pleasantword.com

Also available at:
www.amazon.com
and
www.barnesandnoble.com

Printed in the United States
26858LVS00005B/214-225

9 781414 102917